Headhunter
Confidential

Headhunter
Confidential

THE UNWRITTEN RULES
FOR LANDING A JOB YOU LOVE

Katharine Day Bremer

Ripples Media

"*Headhunter Confidential* could not come at a more urgent time. Kathy Bremer is the best headhunter in the business. She recruited me to the best job ever and helped me attract an extraordinary team. Follow Kathy's advice. It will take you where you need to go."

Paige Alexander
Chief Executive Officer, The Carter Center

"Kathy Bremer reveals the unwritten rules of job hunting with unparalleled clarity, wisdom, and encouragement. She demystifies the hiring process, offering readers a behind-the-scenes look at how top candidates land their dream jobs. What sets this book apart is Kathy's refreshingly human approach. Her emphasis on self-reflection, networking, and strategic positioning turns the job search into an opportunity for personal growth. Each chapter is filled with powerful takeaways, all delivered in an engaging, motivating tone that makes you eager to apply her advice immediately."

Peter Chatel
Director of Operations, Chatel Group; former executive, The Coca-Cola Company; organizational and career coach

"Kathy Bremer helped me hear God's call to joyful ministry at Morningside Presbyterian Church. Her book sparkles with important advice and good humor. It will help you find meaningful work and make you smile along the way."

Rev. Dr. Joanna M. Adams
Former Senior Pastor at Trinity Presbyterian Church and Morningside Presbyterian Church, author, and transformative leader

Published by Ripples Media
www.ripples.media

This work of nonfiction is based on real experiences and people. In order to protect the privacy of individuals, specific names and identifying details have been changed. In some cases, composite characters have been used for clarity. The core facts and intent have been preserved to the best of the author's ability.

First printing 2025

Book and cover design by Burtch Hunter

979-8-9986330-1-0 Paperback
979-8-9986330-2-7 Hardback
979-8-9986330-0-3 Ebook

For Alan, Nick, and Scott

CONTENTS

- Setting your mind on optimism.
- Deciding it's time to move.
- Timing is strategy.
- Positioning yourself if unemployed.
- Choosing a non-traditional path.
- Gauging how long is too long or too short.
- Prioritizing purpose.
- Relating: I've been here.
- Striving for a joy-filled job.

- Thinking differently.
- Identifying what makes you special.
- Living into your animators.
- Owning your strengths.
- Claiming your experience.
- Discerning your purpose.
- Envisioning your next destination.
- Deciding if you should stay put.

- Reaching your destination through people.
- Taking charge by activating relationships.
- Finding helpful people.
- Asking for the right thing.
- Making your contact list.

- Discovering a new trajectory.
- Finding work in a new city.
- Going in warm.
- Relying on contacts.
- Valuing people as your sustainable advantage.
- Creating your plan.

- Discovering the job's bullseye.
- Aiming to hit the bullseye.
- Understanding the larger context.
- Differentiating the bullseye in similar job descriptions.
- Switching sectors.
- Thinking like a hiring committee.
- Working with career gaps.
- Succeeding as an "out of the box" candidate.
- Tailoring a strong resumé.
- Crafting a compelling cover letter.
- Amping up your resumé and cover letter.
- Thinking like a headhunter.
- Realizing it's not all about you.
- Curating your story: a cautionary tale.
- Bringing only your "A" game.
- Gauging your communication.
- Choosing to withdraw or go all in.

- Dissecting a search.
- Prioritizing assets for the current job market.
- Knowing why you fit.
- Telling your unique story.
- Making magic.
- Debunking recruiting myths.
- Translating your why into their what.
- Navigating as an internal candidate.
- Impressing the interview team.

- Preparing for the Top 10 interview questions.
- Inoculating yourself against concerns.
- Following the Top 10 interview tips.
- Curating your references.
- Generating that "something extra."
- Winning over everyone.
- Receiving a job offer.
- Deciding when to say no.
- Owning your power.

RULE NUMBER 6

Love the Journey

- Navigating a satisfying journey.
- Learning from successful job-changing stories.
- Starting strong, with an entry strategy.
- Taking charge of your first few weeks.
- Navigating if your predecessor was beloved.
- Dealing with unexpected disappointment.
- Exiting graciously.
- Building your legacy.
- Choosing to rewire, not retire.
- Loving the journey.

MILESTONE EXERCISES TO GUIDE YOUR SEARCH

FOREWORD

by Bill Novelli

This book, both timeless and urgent, is an excellent blueprint for career success. It is timeless because we all want the job we love, wherever we may be in our careers, from rookies to retirees. It is urgent because we are in a turbulent time, and as I write this, federal government agencies are being downsized and many thousands of employees are searching for new positions. The ripple effect from this surge is causing layoffs and intense competition for jobs in both the civil and private sectors.

I wish I'd had this book with me along my entire career journey, starting at the very beginning. I would have been more prepared, more strategic, and more creative in my search and ultimate choices. *Headhunter Confidential* offers a pathway for everyone, at any stage of your career, in any context. I have given the book with a lecture (OK, not a lecture but a positive message) to each of my grandkids. I'm hopeful.

I've been on both sides of the hiring table: searching for the right job and selecting the best people for jobs. In fact, I'm proud to say I hired Kathy Bremer. I've spent just about half my career in the private sector and half in public service, with a short stint in government. Like Kathy, I believe in what she calls "vertical learning curves, switching your sector of work—say from corporate to nonprofit, or engineering to academia, or government to industry." She assures that "it's almost certain to drive major professional growth."

Kathy is a total pro. She writes, "I've been where some of you are," and she certainly has. When I met her, she was over-seeing the largest account at a major advertising agency in New York. I was the COO at CARE, then the biggest non-government organization (NGO) in the world, working in international relief and development in some 40 countries. I was looking for a SVP for marketing and development (fundraising). I had come from a marketing and advertising background, and I knew about Kathy's impressive accomplishments. In our second interview, she said, in her straight ahead way, "I don't know much, if anything, about fundraising." Now it was my turn to convince her she could do the job and do it well. And she did—very well. Fortunately, I've always been good at hiring people smarter and more talented than I am. It's my super power.

Later, long after I left Porter Novelli, the global communications agency I helped found and build, Kathy left CARE to energize and expand Porter Novelli's Atlanta office. She is truly adept at "vertical learning."

Headhunter Confidential is about winning the job you want. It's about doing your homework in a strategic and grounded way. After all, looking for and landing the ideal job is a big job in itself. What are organizations looking for in a new employee? Examples in this book include: growing revenues, leading strategy change, enhancing visibility and reputation, building teams, and cultivating talent. To achieve those objectives, organizations want technical skills and experience, like accounting, human resources, marketing, and sales.

But there's much more an organization is probably seeking that may not have appeared in the position description. Gallup reports that the five most important traits in demand are motivation, work style, initiative, collaboration, and an analytical approach. Jim Clifton, chairman emeritus at Gallup, says that another important characteristic is being able to reframe problems as opportunities. This is a way to focus on strengths, yours and the organization's.

I also believe that commitment is important: commitment to yourself and to the organizations where you've worked. Have you demonstrated that? Perhaps a situation required all hands on deck to face a crisis of some kind, like a fire or a data hack or an embezzlement. Did you step up and contribute meaningfully to the solution?

Demonstrating your proficiency in relation to the traits reported by Gallup and your commitment to your current or previous organization provide the chance to differentiate yourself from the pack of competitive job seekers. I think a key part of commitment—and something I look for in candidates—is just plain grit. That means courage, resilience in the face of disappointment, constant striving, and tenacity. You aren't going to win every job or every competition in life. I lost a job I cared deeply about and moped for weeks, until my wife said, "You tried your best, get over it." It's been called QTIP (Quit Taking It Personally). I soon moved on to other opportunities. Dan Glickman, former Secretary of Agriculture and a friend, says, "When one door closes, another one opens. But you need to be standing by the door."

A boss told me in my rookie years that you can't always out-think your competition and you can't always outspend them, but you can almost always outwork them. I believe that. Michael Bloomberg, former mayor of New York and a billionaire business owner and philanthropist, believes it, too. He said, "I know what hard work is all about. I'm not the smartest guy, but I can outwork you. It's the one thing I can control." While work-life balance is important, daily hard work pays off.

A fundamental question in this book is Who are you now? It's very difficult to answer that, to look ourselves in the mirror, and to reach a confident conclusion. Honesty is challenging. It's not easy to know, let alone tell ourselves, the truth. While we want to put our best foot forward, we need to deliver on what we commit to. As Kathy says, don't try to sell yourself as something or someone you're not. "Fake it 'til you make it" is seldom a good strategy.

You need to know when you're in the wrong place and leave rather than keep pushing and grinding without success. A healthy work culture, where employees can succeed individually and collectively through teamwork, is probably the most important aspect of job satisfaction. Kathy details how a toxic culture can destroy morale. Talented people gravitate to organizations that offer ample opportunities to excel, advance, and feel positive about their work.

A simple working definition of culture is "the way we do things around here." Sometimes it's the boss who is toxic rather than the whole organization, thus the saying that employees tend to quit supervisors rather than organizations. I once had a boss, a division VP, who was brilliant, but he humiliated people. I learned two lessons from him: how not to treat others and the art of marketing. I thought of it as "reverse mentoring." Treating people well should be obvious and can be a personal and competitive advantage. A major example of fleeing a bad work culture is a woman I admire: former U.S. Senator Olympia Snowe of Maine. She decided, after much contemplation and discussion with trusted colleagues, that the Senate was no longer a place where key issues facing the country could be resolved. So she left.

Kathy stresses throughout this book that we will reach our destination, whatever it may be, through people—"your sustainable advantage." The people we already know and those we meet on this journey will make the difference by providing advice, making introductions (so we're "going in warm, not cold"), providing references, serving as mentors and coaches, and offering a shoulder to lean on.

Finding the right job, like so much else in life, is built on relationships. As Kathy points out, we need to network and maintain these relationships over time, not just when we need them. Moreover, this is not a one-way street. We can pay that generosity back by helping others, often those younger and less experienced in the field. That's why she spends so much time helping with career coaching and making connections.

I enjoy the opportunity to mentor up-and-comers. In my decade-plus teaching in the MBA program at Georgetown, I've come to believe that tomorrow's leaders are sitting in our classrooms today. Alumni check in with me frequently to tell me how they're doing. Some of their questions make me wish I could have given them this book years ago.

One student came to see me and said, "I'm graduating next week. What's the pathway to success?" I replied, "There isn't one. There's no single pathway. The challenge and the joy are in the journey." As Kathy would have said, "Love the journey, and it will love you back." Another student told me, "I'm graduating and, confidentially, I don't know anything!" How do you answer that? I said, "It's OK, I don't know anything either." I'm not sure if that gave him confidence to overcome his imposter syndrome. They both would have benefited from reading what you have in your hands.

Kathy stresses purpose, which she says can matter most of all in aligning what you care deeply about with what you do—or want to do—for a living. An organization with a meaningful purpose can energize and inspire. I find that younger people are often purpose-driven. They often say they want purpose with a paycheck. One graduate told me, "I have student debt. I need to pay it off, and I want to have a good career and a family, but I never want to lose my sense of purpose." So think hard about your values in your job search. I find that, with the right fit, you can find purpose in any sector.

Be prepared to hit the bullseye as Kathy describes in this book. What is the organization looking for and how can you match up to land the job? The first person to win over is the headhunter. Preparation for this, as well as for later stages, is critical. Imagine you're talking to Kathy Bremer. Show her you understand the prospective organization's purpose and mission. Tell her how you can add value. And go a step further by telling her about—or at least inquiring about—their competitors, partners, and other stakeholders. Be curious. Demonstrate that you're a learner.

Storytelling is a valuable way to connect, but be sure to craft a strategic story that promotes your accomplishments and underscores your commitment. Vulnerability and humility help.

Don't be arrogant or self-serving in your story. Kathy will want to hear your "elevator speech"—a short description of yourself and your competence for the job. Make it a good one, and vary it a bit as you move through the process so you don't sound like a robot on repeat. While you want to show passion for the opportunity, beware of overdoing it.

Kathy points out that securing an interview is often the most challenging part of the process. Her top ten interview questions are an excellent framework to help you prepare. Sometimes search committees and headhunters will throw you a curve ball—in the dirt. Here are some I've encountered:

- What framework do you use to write a plan?
- What haven't you accomplished that you wish you had?
- I hear you're not warm and fuzzy (Yes, this was how a major search committee member started a key interview with me. I said, "Well, I'm warm.").
- What was the first time you had a vision for something that others thought couldn't be done, and how did you bring them along?
- What do you do for fun? (This can be a chance to stand out. Co-ed street hockey, coaching Little League, opera, chairing a nonprofit?)

You'll want to rehearse, ideally with a colleague. Be ready, be substantive, and be unique. One way to get a leg up is "working retail" to really understand the organization you're interviewing. By that, I mean tour their hospital or clinic, shop in their out-lets, talk to a sales rep, read their fundraising mailings, or check out their competitors. A friend took a job as a Walmart cashier for several months just to talk to customers about their health issues so she could begin a relevant start-up.

As *Headhunter Confidential* points out, entering a search as an internal candidate comes with its own challenges. I've been there twice and won one and lost one. Yes, you know everything about the organization, but you're not new and shiny. The challenge is to show exceptional potential. You know where things stand. Now lay out your vision for where things can go, and provide internal references and champions without it coming off like a campaign.

Some people keep working late into their careers out of necessity. Others might retire early or at a typical age. Kathy says she is in her "final career" at BoardWalk. Is she going to stop working and only play golf and cards? Or take up part-time work and volunteering and other pursuits? She advises us not to "retire," but to "rewire" with a plan to reinvent ourselves for new adventures. I have a "retirement" business card from a friend who did it the "rocking chair on the front porch" way. The card reads: "Retired, ask someone else, no deadlines, no business, not my problem." That's not for Kathy, nor for me, and I expect not for anyone who wants to stay active and replicate Kathy's pursuit of purpose and joy. Life's key question is, "What's next?" This book will certainly help you figure that out.

Bill Novelli is a professor emeritus at the McDonough School of Business at Georgetown University. He was CEO of AARP, the Campaign for Tobacco-Free Kids, and Porter Novelli, the global PR firm. His latest book is *Good Business: The Talk, Fight, Win Way to Change the World.*

Time for Change

Welcome to *Headhunter Confidential.* I bet you've opened this book because you're ready to change jobs or you're considering it. Perhaps a change has been forced upon you—or is about to be. You might be ready for more challenges, more growth opportunities, or more meaningful work. Maybe you're just starting out in your career or restarting after a gap.

Whether your change is driven by you, or by someone or something else, a time of transition is a time of opportunity. And if you want to land in a job you love, you've come to the right place.

Today we live in a post-career era, where each of us must chart our own career path. Internships and jobs with health insurance are rare, as are long tenures at a single company. Continual growth and experience are the currencies of a satisfying career. Each of us encounters log jams, stagnation, or misalignment, and at some point most of us are forced out of work.

Change is inevitable, and it can feel daunting—especially when it's foisted upon us. We may struggle to find our footing. I wrote this book to help you take advantage of your transitions to chart your next great adventures.

Headhunter Confidential reveals the unwritten rules that only headhunters and successful job seekers know. It shares the secrets I've learned from eighteen years as a headhunter, five personal career transitions, and the hundreds of people I've coached and placed in jobs along the way. I know what it takes to succeed at job-hunting, and the joy of having work that aligns with your values, strengths, and purpose.

I'm excited to share the unwritten rules, and the dos and don'ts, for winning in today's job market. You will read stories of everyday people on journeys like yours and find out how they pursued and secured rewarding positions. The names and details are changed, but their stories are real. The unwritten rules for landing work you love are:

- Adopt the right mindset.
- Set a clear direction.
- Connect with people.
- Focus on the bullseye.
- Stand out to stand apart.
- Love the journey.

You don't need to settle for a job that doesn't give you joy. *Headhunter Confidential* will take you on a refreshing journey to your next great opportunity. *Let's get started!*

Headhunter
Confidential

Adopt the Right Mindset

Close your eyes and picture how it will feel to wake up each day excited to begin your work. Your job lines up with your talents, passion, and purpose. You are impactful and aligned with the goals, values, and people.

How does that feel? You show up as your authentic self. You are respected by your colleagues. You spend minimal time on office politics, superfluous tasks, or things you're just not good at (we all have them). No one expects you to compromise your integrity or health. You experience your job as meaningful and enjoyable.

The gap between a job you love and one you endure is the difference between excitement and clock watching. The journey to a great new position can be energizing, in and of itself. The first rule of successful job hunting is: Adopt the right mindset.

Launching a job search evokes feelings that can range from exhilaration to terror. If you were laid off or sidelined, anger and fear are natural responses.

Process and learn what you can from the experience, with the help of friends, family, and colleagues. Processing is the first step of a positive transition. Create the space you need to work through anger and disappointment before embarking on a job search, because those emotions can sap your energy and sabotage forward movement.

You deserve a job that aligns with your talents, passion, and purpose.

Try not to let the past live rent-free in your mind for too long. It takes an optimistic mindset to envision a new future and connect effectively with people who can help you navigate the path to your next great adventure.

Kristine's story demonstrates how a job search is hampered by lingering negativity:

> Kristine had thrived as the leader of the fundraising team at a large, respected nonprofit. Under her leadership, the team regularly exceeded its revenue goals. Everything was going well until the global pandemic hit and people dispersed to their homes, separated from one another and the seamless collaboration Kristine had cultivated. Fundraising events were cancelled, momentum languished, and donations dropped. Kristine struggled to lead the dispersed team. The group's

results and cohesion suffered. The organization's revenue plummeted.

As financial challenges escalated, Kristine's job was eliminated. She was devastated. As a leader accustomed to accolades, she felt defeated and diminished. As a single mother, she despaired at the loss of her salary. A few weeks' severance hardly made a difference.

Kristine called me. As she shared her story, anger and resentment tumbled out, tears flowed, and her voice cracked as she recounted details. I fully empathized with her feelings of trauma, rejection, and fear.

As a headhunter, however, I was worried. Kristine was experiencing intense emotions in reaction to being fired, understandably. But by letting her resentment spill over, she was telegraphing a lack of readiness to move forward.

Setting your mind on optimism.

—

As I thought through my conversation with Kristine, I realized her effort to find the next job would be stymied by her mindset. She needed to work through her feelings of anger and fear. Until then, she would be unable to muster the focus and optimism essential to a successful search.

Check your mindset at the outset of a job search. Pause to process feelings of worry, anger, and insecurity. Enlist family, colleagues, and counselors to deal with what has happened. Move to a point where you can compartmentalize those feelings in order to reframe your job search as "looking for my next adventure." How you imagine your search will impact how you plan, how you act, and how others respond to you. A negative mindset, even if you try to hide it, can color your interactions and openness to opportunities.

> I called Kristine back. With compassion, I asked questions, listened, and gave her honest feedback. I reminded her of her stellar record and abundant talent. I observed that her resentment was darkening her thinking and would hamper her job search. I suggested she find a way to process what had happened and to emerge with optimism about her future.
>
> Kristine took my advice. She didn't rush into a job hunt. Using her severance as a bridge, she sought advice and support from family and friends, spent quality time with her children, and transitioned from resentment to acceptance of the situation. Gradually, Kristine adjusted her mindset and began to imagine finding her next great opportunity.

A successful job-hunting journey begins when you're ready to move *forward* to something new, rather than *away* from a bad situation. Adjusting your mindset requires time, validation from people you trust, and sometimes professional counseling. Here are some strategies to try:

- Write about what happened and your feelings about it.
- Think as objectively as you can about the events and circumstances. Try to put yourself in others' shoes.
- Process your reactions with trusted friends.
- Ask for their suggestions about what they think you're

best at and should do next.

- Compose a list of your accomplishments.
- Identify your strengths that drove those accomplishments and the times your work has brought you joy.
- Work with a career coach or therapist and begin to envision what comes next.

---

*Move toward a new adventure,
rather than away from a bad situation.*

By resolving issues of resentment, anger, and self-doubt, you're changing your inner dialogue and moving to a mindset that's optimistic and forward-looking. Imagine a situation that would excite you, draw upon your strengths, and align with your purpose. Begin to embrace confidence and excitement about what might come next.

Deciding it's time to move.

—

The time to seek a new opportunity can be driven by you or outside forces. It's time for a change if you are facing one or more of these situations:

- You're out of work, downsized, forced out, or about to be.
- The work culture is toxic.
- You have a values or work mismatch.
- You're bored, feeling stuck, or in need of fresh challenges.

- New life circumstances call for something different.
- You're re-starting after a gap.
- You're just starting out.

The source of your next great opportunity can be found inside of you.

Transitions can feel overwhelming, uncertain, and scary. Getting a great new job can feel like a daunting task, especially when you are currently out of work or in a challenging work circumstance. You may be sure it's time to move but uncertain what you want to do next, or what opportunities could be available. No matter what is driving your change, you will find your next opportunity by following the proven process in this book.

What is leading you to make a change? Are you yearning for more challenging work, more opportunities to grow, more compensation, or a more aligned work situation? Are you out of work or facing imminent disruption or termination?

Crisis *is* opportunity.

You may relate to the Chinese proverb, "A crisis is an opportunity riding the dangerous wind." A career crisis feels dangerous, or at least risky. No matter how difficult your current situation may be, you can and will find a wonderful next opportunity. Just as the Chinese character for "opportunity" is found inside the character for "crisis," the source of your next great opportunity can be found inside of you.

Whether change is being driven by you, a bad situation, or a pink slip, I hope you will embrace the transition as a positive turning point in your life and career.

危机 The Chinese symbol for Change. The word is Wei Ji (way jee), with Ji translated as "turning point."

No matter the cause, you can take charge and create the future you want. The truth is that regardless of where your journey starts, the unwritten rules in this book provide a roadmap to a great next chapter. While the starting point of your journey is unique and the drivers of change differ, the secrets I share will take you where you want to go. They will work for you on this move and for moves later in your career when your priorities have evolved.

Job transitions have many different starting points. You may relate to one or more of these stories about real people who navigated change and landed a job they love.

Facing a termination.

—

Displacement can result from a layoff, firing, or forced resignation. The cause can be a merger, a budget cut, a new manager, a restructure, an indefinite furlough, or some other situation. Circumstances beyond our control force change, and we have to somehow adjust and move forward.

This change can be sudden. Other times, we may be able to delay or mitigate it to give ourselves time or space.

Meet Drew. After fifteen years in his company, he was assigned a new manager and then, in short order, received a pink slip. Here's the painful first chapter of Drew's story.

Drew was respected and valued within his company as "the fixer." He was known for tackling intractable assignments. He was often deployed to a chaotic department or tasked with untangling tough budget or personnel issues. Feisty and determined, Drew relished the tough assignments and would work around the clock until problems were resolved. He never ran out of assignments.

The unwritten rules will help you get to where you want to go.

That was until a new manager took over the department and Drew found himself sidelined. The new boss made no effort to connect with Drew and didn't value his history of successes. When Drew and his problem-solving skills were no longer being celebrated and shared with other departments, the pink slip followed.

Having survived several rounds of layoffs and watched other loyal staff depart, Drew was caught off guard now that it was his turn. He felt overwhelmed. The timing of his departure was to be immediate. The answer on severance was "talk to HR." Five minutes after it began, the meeting with his new boss ended. Drew shuffled back to his office to call HR and pack up his laptop, knick-knacks, and awards.

"What now?" he thought. Then he remembered to email friends at the company with his mobile number and personal email. He tried to capture critical contact information before the company cut off his email access. He wondered whether it was possible to negotiate for more time, given his tenure and track record.

Don't forget to negotiate!

Drew initially saw only one solution: to accept the company's severance offer and walk away. After some reflection, he felt he was owed more for the loyalty and value he had brought to the company. He knew his track record was meaningful and his contributions should entitle him to better than a rushed departure. He decided to fight.

Drew proposed a handful of final projects, which enabled him to negotiate a later departure date. That gave him a chance to stay financially whole for a few more weeks, finish projects he'd started, and say proper goodbyes to longtime colleagues. It also gave him a better head start on considering next career options.

Fleeing a toxic culture.

—

Many of us have experienced a work culture that feels toxic. We've witnessed low collegiality and support, a sense of competition and gamesmanship, and a lack of team cohesion and shared goals. A work environment can become toxic as a result of poor management, a challenging merger, unclear corporate values or practices, major layoffs or restructuring, uncertainty, or unwanted change.

A toxic environment can cause problems for your well-being and must be addressed. Angela endured a toxic environment for several months before taking action:

Angela woke up every Monday with a sense of dread about the week. A new manager was piling on expectations that felt unreasonable, and the culture had turned toxic. Staff groups were becoming increasingly siloed. Incidents of micro-aggression were on the rise. Her health was suffering, as she experienced headaches and episodes of nausea.

Angela knew she had to escape, but with her daughter close to college age and her mother fighting cancer, Angela could not afford to be out of work, even temporarily. She had to find a way to stay while plotting a safe escape to a new job.

She decided to have a heart-to-heart conversation with her new manager to try to improve the situation. She carefully rehearsed her words, determined to make this a positive interaction. At the meeting, she began by naming what she appreciated, then explained the challenging current dynamics, including her own experiences. She asked for help in creating a more collaborative, supportive work environment and provided suggestions on how they might do that. The manager committed to putting more emphasis on inclusive culture and holding people accountable for their actions.

This gave Angela space to recover her physical and mental health. She achieved the desired outcome: a positive discussion with her manager and the manager's commitment to help change the culture. She began to enjoy work more and continued her tenure for a few months as she navigated to a new job.

How to change a toxic work environment.

Don't be afraid to speak up and try to improve the situation. Sometimes it takes head-on communication to recruit help in repairing a toxic culture. Before you speak up, be clear about the outcome you want and thoughtfully consider your words and affect. Keep the focus on potential solutions rather than complaints.

Here are ways to improve a toxic work situation:

- Analyze what is making the environment toxic (e.g., lack of collaboration, poor communication, internal politics). Seek clarity about the root causes. What needs to change for the situation to improve?

- Model the change you want to see. Proactively collaborate and help colleagues. Encourage and reward teamwork. Publicly recognize others' contributions. Generously give credit to others. Express gratitude.

- Build one-on-one relationships and trust by forging meaningful connections. Find allies who share your interest in creating a healthier work environment.

- Propose regular team meetings. Make them a safe

and supportive opportunity for discussion. Invite others to contribute to the agenda.

- Look for areas of alignment and call out progress as it happens.
- Maintain a diplomatic tone when raising concerns or offering feedback.

Remember to take care of yourself. Know your own limits and protect your personal time. Engage in activities outside of work that generate positive energy.

Changing a toxic environment is possible, but it takes time. Sometimes outside facilitation can accelerate the diagnosis of the situation and prescribe possible solutions. If specific individuals are making the environment toxic, management needs to hold them accountable to change. Alternatively, they may need to exit the organization.

If departure is your only option, before you signal your intention, figure out the timing that will work best for you. Give your supervisor a plan that protects you and the organization and commit to a positive transition. Negotiate a mutually acceptable plan and date of departure. Agree on a final set of deliverables. If they ask you to leave sooner than you wish, be proactive in negotiating fair timing and severance.

Try to maintain a positive relationship with your organization. Future employers will contact your current organization for references. A collegial relationship matters and benefits you over time.

Escaping a mismatch.

—

Selena's values were at odds with those of her organization. She knew she had to find another place to work. Here's her story:

Selena often asked herself, "Why am I continuing to work here?" Her company was in the oil and gas business, and she was acutely aware of climate change issues and the impacts of fossil fuel pollution on children and families in less affluent communities like where she grew up.

As part of Selena's marketing job, she helped communicate the company's perspectives. Her job was to advocate for the company's priorities, enhance its visibility and reputation, and defend the industry.

Selena increasingly felt a values mismatch. She realized that she was working to advance an industry that didn't align with her values and purpose. While she had never specifically defined her purpose, she knew it was not consistent with her company's goals. At the same time, the compensation and benefits were excellent. She worried that she couldn't make enough money at a different organization whose purpose might be a better fit for her.

Knowing her ideal work would address some kind of human or global need, Selena decided to learn more about the nonprofit landscape and to more clearly define her own strengths and purpose before beginning her job search.

Yearning to grow.

—

In the first few months of a new job, you are climbing the proverbial mountain to understand the organization and your own responsibilities. Once you fully grasp the new role, you begin to notch accomplishments and expand your contributions. If you're fortunate, your responsibilities and growth will evolve for years to come.

At some point, though, you may sense your personal and professional growth have stalled. You may feel you've reached a dead end. If so, you may grow bored and restless. When this begins to happen, seek opportunities that promise greater excitement and challenge. Could your talents and passion be deployed in a different context within the organization? That is the first path to explore.

If you find limited possibilities to grow where you are, explore opportunities outside your organization, as Sally did:

> For the third day in a row, Sally woke up thinking, "I don't feel like working today." She forced herself out of bed and turned on her computer. Her busy schedule was filled with activities and meetings to address problems she'd worked on for years. None of it excited her anymore. After a decade in a role she had mostly enjoyed, Sally was no longer animated by the work and its challenges. She was not constantly learning or experimenting with new ideas.
>
> To stimulate personal growth, Sally had attended outside conferences and taken advantage of training opportunities. She'd also been volunteering with a local nonprofit organization.

But she realized she wanted more from her work. "I don't have any more ways to grow at this organization," she thought. She decided to undertake a job search.

When you're no longer growing and feel like opportunities have evaporated where you are, start planning a move. In my case, after a fast-paced decade in the advertising world at two different agencies, I found myself working on the agency's largest account with no viable options for new roles or challenges. That realization set me on a path to find my next career, which led me to a whole different sector.

When one door closes, push others open.

Drew had not been seeking a change. He had worked in different positions over his fifteen years at the company and had enjoyed most of the challenges put before him. He had been loyal, positive, and productive. He did not feel ready to leave, yet he was forced to go.

After several days of airing his disappointment with his spouse and friends, Drew woke up to an unscheduled Monday and an unknown future. He knew it is harder to find a job when you're out of work. He wasn't sure what he wanted to do now or even what to do next. To be honest, he was angry. And confused. And worried. His husband challenged him: "You did fine work at that company. What do you want to do next?"

Drew decided to take time to regroup and talk with mentors and others, including several friends who had been laid off recently as well. He asked for advice and for referrals to others who might share their creative ideas. Through his meetings with a variety of people, Drew began to formulate possible new directions.

Addressing life changes.

—

Life circumstances influence our career aspirations. Among these are a change in location, an illness, a new addition to the family, parents in need of care, or new priorities. After several decades in finance at one company, Joe decided he wanted to make more of a difference in the final stages of his career:

> Joe was a senior financial manager in a company with healthy revenues where he could have worked until retirement. The organization had no ambitious plans on the horizon, and Joe realized his growth and learning curve had flattened. While his relatively high compensation was enabling the family to save for college tuition, that was almost completed and he no longer felt compelled to earn at the same level. He realized that the challenges of his position and the prospects of his organization no longer excited him.
>
> Joe felt he had one more big job in him. He felt an urge to put his skills to work in an organization that was helping people in need. He had no idea where to begin, but he began the process of exploration.

Re-starting after a gap.

—

Many people experience gaps during their careers, maybe due to family illness, a layoff, a decision to prioritize parenting, a tough job-hunting climate, or a relocation. Re-entering the job market calls for special strategies since potential employers may wonder whether your skills are current or if your level of stamina, pace, and energy are commensurate with their needs. Also, the pool of competitive candidates will include people whose resumés show no gaps.

Michelle was returning to full-time work after caring for sick parents and a newborn. Her four-year gap was explainable; however, it made her less competitive relative to others seeking the same jobs.

In addition to providing a brief, clear explanation of why she left her former job and her years as a caregiver, Michelle employed a range of strategies to establish her relevance and readiness to work, including:

- Gaining access to opportunities through referrals so interviewers already had a positive impression of her talents.

- Proactively including a detailed explanation of her gap as part of a self-introduction that emphasized relevant work accomplishments and passion for the position.

- Citing specifics on how she has maintained or advanced her knowledge of the field (e.g. courses, certifications, volunteer work).

- Doing in-depth homework about each opportunity to

demonstrate knowledge and interest.

- Providing names of references who could speak to any concerns, including individuals known to the hiring team.

Just getting started.

—

When you're first starting out, securing a first job can feel intimidating. You may be tempted to generate a sense of forward motion by applying to numerous postings online or sending your resumé to individuals you research online. As hard as you work to tailor your resumé and include the right keywords to impress the ATS (applicant tracking system), electronic applications often fall into a black hole. You don't know whether your application was received. You receive zero feedback from the potential employer or the market.

Gordon plunged into a job search while graduating during an economic recession. With a liberal arts degree and light prior work experience, he was competing with millions of other graduates seeking entry-level work. To secure a foothold in the working world, he expected to make some compromises, but he hoped to find his way to a position in his general field of study.

My advice to Gordon was to identify two or three areas of interest and seek the advice of his professors, family, friends, and people in that field. His response: "But I'm an introvert."

Nonetheless, he was generating minimal response from his online efforts. He reluctantly began reaching out and connecting with people his parents, professors, and advisors suggested.

Tentative and reticent at first, Gordon became emboldened by people's willingness to help him. Two months later, he landed the job of his dreams.

Timing is strategy.

—

You know you're ready to make a change, but stop to think about the consequences of moving too fast. Remember that being currently employed is reassuring to potential employers, who are generally risk averse. While a job hunt takes time and adds to your workload, job hunting while unemployed puts you at a disadvantage. If you're out of work, you'll spend precious time explaining why.

When possible, remain in your current situation for the duration of your job search. To give yourself time for an effective search, carve out time on evenings and weekends to build your plan. One strategy for extending your stay in your current organization is to identify new ways to add value or to refresh your role. Joan confronted the need to extend her tenure, despite being displaced from the work she loved:

> The news hit Joan like a bolt of lightning. "The company is being acquired." Joan's heart sank as her manager explained that her role was going to change from the project management role she excelled at to a sales job she didn't want. Her choices were to leave or to take a job that did not fit her strengths.
>
> Joan proposed a compromise: She would spend half her time on the external sales mandate and the other half developing leads for the sales team. The

latter role played to her strengths. She believed she could provide value relative to achieving the growth goals. While she and her manager implemented this short-term solution, Joan gained the time to develop the path to her next opportunity.

Positioning yourself if unemployed.

—

If you're between work opportunities or have a gap in your resumé, prepare for the inevitable questions from hiring committees about why. Hiring managers often have concerns if a candidate is not currently employed. They speculate: Why did this candidate leave their job (really)? Is this individual hard to work with? Why was their position eliminated? Does the gap mean they're less ready for this job than a candidate who's currently working?

To inoculate yourself against speculation, offer a clear, upfront explanation.

To inoculate yourself against such speculation, offer a clear, upfront explanation. Design your explanation to anticipate and override potential concerns.

When Oliver began his recent job hunt, he was unemployed. Within the first few minutes of every interview, he made a point of explaining why: "My previous organization had a leadership change. The new CEO wanted a fresh start, and that makes sense.

I realized the timing was right for me to move to my next adventure."

Depending on your circumstances and facts, other answers might include:

- I needed to take time out to care for my sick mother in a different city. That situation is now resolved, and I'm excited to get back to work.

- Our company was sold, and I took the chance to fulfill my dream of traveling around the world. I've returned and am eager to jump back in.

- Our family relocated due to my partner's career opportunity. We took a few months to settle the family, and I'm excited to return to work.

- I decided to try my hand at consulting. While the work was fulfilling, I missed collaborating with teams and being part of a larger organization and purpose.

If your time gap is significant (more than a few months), include in your resumé any consulting, educational, or volunteer activities you pursued. This demonstrates that you have continued to maintain and grow your abilities.

Choosing a non-traditional path.

—

If you are entrepreneurial by nature or have several directions you want to pursue, you may decide that your best path is something other than a full-time position. Entrepreneurs often choose independence, freedom, and the ability to innovate over a job in an organization. They develop more than one stream of revenue and build a "portfolio career."

Discovering what you're meant to do, as part of mastering Rule Number 2, will help you discern your best options and income potentials. It will help you identify your strengths, purpose, and potential direction. You may want to combine freelance work, such as writing, teaching, or consulting, with paid ongoing positions. Play it safe by developing at least one reliable income stream. If you have a talent you're developing into a business, you might combine that with teaching on the subject.

Connecting with people is critical to gaining traction in your selected areas. Once you determine the streams you want to cultivate, identify people both inside and outside your network whose advice will help you advance. In Rule Number 3, we explore how people we turn to for advice often turn into valuable business relationships.

Gauging how long is too long or too short.

—

Hiring committees are wary of candidates who change jobs often (every one to three years). They surmise that the individual is unlikely to stay for long at this job either. They recognize the high cost of employee turnover, both in financial resources and momentum. As a rule of thumb, the cost of hiring a new staff member is twice the departing individual's salary. In addition, they consider the opportunity cost of lost know-how and organizational familiarity. In general, hiring committees prefer people with multi-year tenures. Averaging four to eight years in each position is often viewed as ideal. Several years of tenure implies accomplishments and stability.

How long is too long in a job? Hiring committees appreciate candidates who demonstrate staying power, but tenures longer than fifteen years may raise concerns about whether you can adapt to a new setting. While there are no hard and fast rules, ten to fifteen years at the same organization, particularly with a record of promotions and different assignments, is generally viewed positively. Hiring teams value breadth of experience and adaptability. They look for evidence of professional growth and exposure to risks and challenges.

The happy medium tenure is four to eight years. Most hiring teams look favorably at candidates who have spent four to ten years in one or more recent positions. That range demonstrates commitment to a job, plus adaptability and professional momentum. After about the twelve-year mark in one organization, unless you have had significant promotions or changes in responsibilities, hiring committees may wonder about your ability to adapt to their unique environment. They will be curious as to why you have stayed in one job that long. You can reassure them by demonstrating how you have been growing and gaining a wide range of experience throughout your tenure.

Among the assets hiring committees and managers value:

- Breadth of experience signals an ability to handle diverse issues, problems, and cultural contexts.

- A hybrid background, including stints across more than one sector (e.g. corporate, nonprofit, government, academic) is seen as beneficial as long as it includes experience in or adjacent to the hiring team's sector.

- An upward career trajectory is prized. Evidence of this can be sequential promotions, demonstrated growth or other accomplishments, and results. The trajectory can be within one or several organizations.

Prioritizing purpose.

—

Job satisfaction comes easily when your role centers your areas of interest, challenges that animate you, and your sense of purpose. Naming your strengths and discovering what you're meant to do provides a filter for evaluating new directions. Aligning who you are with what you do for a living truly matters. If your job and your purpose are at odds, or if what you do best is not what your job requires, your tenure will be shorter, less joyful, and less impactful.

How you leave is as important as how you arrive.
Your career is made up of sequential opportunities. How you exit your current work affects your future. As you seek your next opportunity, be strategic about how and when you depart. Be sure you:

- Give fair notice, ideally more than is required, still allowing for time off between jobs.
- Help plan your organization's transition.
- Honor your commitments in substance and spirit.
- Avoid burning bridges with people at your current employer.
- Consider who in your organization will provide references for you.

- Design and execute a positive exit strategy.

  Questions to ask yourself as you consider making a change:

- Instead of leaving now, can I buy time by reconfiguring my role or negotiating interesting new responsibilities here?

- How might I increase the value I add to this organization to increase my longevity or impact?

The happy medium is four to eight years.

- What's my legacy here? Have I completed what I came here to do? Have I developed a successor and a succession plan?

- How can I transition out in a way that keeps me whole, respects the organization, and sets me up for future success?

- Can I negotiate favorable terms when I depart: timing, severance, and the nature of the announcement?

- Who here will be a good reference for me?

- When and how shall I tell my manager I'm departing in a way that maintains a positive relationship and paves the way for an amicable transition?

- How can I orchestrate a gracious departure and ongoing connection?

Relating: I've been here.

—

I have embarked on five change journeys over the course of my career. I've worked in five diverse sectors and professions. Each turning point, each season of change, was unique and led to something exciting. In some instances, I drove the change. In others, the time for change presented itself in the form of external factors outside my control, such as a new boss or a new organizational direction I didn't choose to take.

During these changes, I have experienced feelings that ranged from hopeless, trapped, and anxious to hopeful, confident, and excited. Some elements of my eclectic corporate and nonprofit career journey may resonate with you. Here is the short version of my story:

Soon after college, I boarded a one-way flight from my hometown in New York to Tokyo, Japan. I'd been hired by a Japanese company as an English teacher and writer. As the plane touched down 6700 miles from my home, I thought: "This could be a great adventure or a miserable experience. Either way, it will mean personal and professional growth."

My career in Tokyo offered steep growth opportunities and challenges. I'm glad I took the risk to move overseas and to live and work in a whole new culture. I had so much to learn, including a new language, which gave me a vertical learning curve. I grew in ways I could never have imagined. I worked for a small trading company, then a large Japanese company you've heard of: Canon. I had a chance to write for *Newsweek*, to contribute to a book on Japanese culture, and to edit international radio news copy for English-language radio broadcasts.

My first career in Tokyo was life-changing. I immersed

myself in new ideas, opportunities, and culture and benefitted from experiences and relationships that would have never happened had I remained in my comfort zone. But I didn't want to live my life so far away from home. I wondered whether I could find my way to a job in New York. With "If you can make it there, you can make it anywhere…" playing silently in my head, I returned to New York.

> *Each time, change took me to a more satisfying role.*

Back in New York, I eventually started my second career as an account executive at a Madison Avenue advertising agency. A fast-paced, enjoyable decade passed with demanding clients and several promotions, including one while I was on maternity leave. Then I began to realize my learning curve was flattening. I still enjoyed the work, but I was leading the agency's largest account with no other opportunities on the horizon. As my excitement and learning curve dwindled, I decided to search for my next adventure.

The feeling of restlessness told me it was time for a change. I had loved volunteering in the industry and in the community and thought my next opportunities could be in marketing or nonprofit work. I reached out to people in my network for advice.

My third career was in nonprofits. One of my advisors introduced me to CARE, an international nonprofit, and I was hired as SVP of marketing and fundraising. That job came with a staff of 125 (versus the eight on my advertising team), global travel, a family relocation to Atlanta, and a mission that fueled my passion. The learning curve was steep. Over several years the curve flattened, and as my children reached the ages of 7 and 12, I realized I needed a job with less travel and fewer 60-hour work weeks. (My younger son later complained, "You spent my childhood in Rwanda." Ouch!).

For my fourth career, I sought an opportunity in my hometown. Once again, I relied on people. Through my network, I found an exciting next role as general manager of the Atlanta office of Porter Novelli, a global public relations agency. While a corporate entity, Porter Novelli had a mission: "doing well by doing good." The clients we served were organizations that advanced health, equity, and other important causes. Our office achieved tenfold growth, and we built a diverse, highly-engaged team. After a joyful eight years, I decided to seek a new adventure at a time of headquarters management changes. Again, my network guided me to my next adventure.

My fifth and current career as a headhunter began eighteen years ago when I joined BoardWalk Consulting as an executive search consultant. I'm still learning, growing, and loving the job. I work with wonderful organizations to recruit and prepare the leaders who will help them achieve their aspirations. I have the privilege of coaching numerous candidates and helping them find and win work they love.

Over the course of my career, I have switched jobs for different reasons: a desire for growth, greater alignment, or a sense that cultural, management, or other conditions made the timing ripe for a change.

At each turning point, I followed roughly the rules in this book, fine-tuning along the way based on experience. At each turn, I paused before job-seeking to assess my strengths, motivations, and purpose. Then I turned to people for advice and referrals. When the right opportunity presented itself, I used the strategies in the book to stand out among other candidates, while maintaining good relationships with people in my current organization. Each time, change took me to a more satisfying role. As an added bonus (pun intended), in all but one career change, my compensation increased.

Striving for a joy-filled job.

—

I've seen hundreds of people secure the job of a lifetime. I've also seen people settle for positions that weren't a good match for their strengths or purpose. Too often, I've seen talented individuals fall short of winning the job of their dreams. Despite their qualifications and best efforts, they didn't get chosen. In some cases, this was because they jumped headlong into a search without assessing their strengths and purpose and without knowing the unwritten rules. They might have received an offer if only they'd known the secrets in this book.

If you're like most people, you don't have an exact answer to the question, "What are my strengths, interests, and life purpose?" You may not currently have an answer to the question, "Where can I best apply my abilities and passion?" The contours of your ideal job will become clearer as you follow the unwritten rules and process outlined in this book. You will enhance your understanding of your uniqueness and how that shapes the opportunities you should pursue. You will envision your next opportunity and use the rules presented here to plot a strategic and fulfilling job search.

TOP TAKEAWAYS

Dos and don'ts for your search.

Dos

- Take charge of your future. Go for a job that gives you joy.

- Think strategically. Focus, be intentional, create a plan (rather than rushing).

- Think long-term. Build relationships. Go for win-win transitions.

Don'ts

- Don't start looking for a new job without a positive mindset and sense of direction.

- Don't underestimate the importance of discerning your purpose and what animates you before you start a search.

- Don't leave, if possible, without a next opportunity in place. Avoid short job stints (two years or less).

Set a Clear Direction

You're ready for a change. You may be more than ready, but your first step is not looking for a job! It's looking inside yourself.

Most people launch a job hunt without pausing to analyze their strengths and what animates them. They update their social media presence and resumé, scan job sites, and amp up attendance at networking events. They may begin applying to a number of different job openings. While these can be useful activities, they are scattershot and time-wasting if you're unsure where you want to end up. After expending considerable energy, you can wind up without a job or in a position you're not excited about.

Before you jump into job-search mode, consider this: Work consumes close to half your waking weekday hours—35+ hours a week, about 245 days a year. If you want to spend those hours doing what you love and do best, you need a plan. Starting a job search without preparation is like embarking on a trip without a destination. Begin your search with an "inside journey" that helps you clarify what your perfect job looks like and move in that direction.

Starting a job search without preparation is like embarking on a trip without a destination.

The risks of jumping into job-search mode without first taking your "inside journey" include:

Chasing jobs that aren't a good match. It's easy to confuse activity with forward motion. You risk wasting valuable time pursuing opportunities that your inside journey might rule out as low-potential.

Mistaking a job offer for the right job. If you say yes to a job that only partially matches your potential, the mismatch may lead to discontent, a slowdown in your growth, or a premature departure.

Missing the boat on a perfect opportunity. If you chase opportunities that are outside your areas of strength, you may miss out on opportunities that are a better fit. Don't waste your energy pursuing jobs that are a long shot or outside your core interests.

Thinking differently.

—

People who land a job they love look inside themselves for answers before jumping into an external job search. They consider questions like, "Who am I now? What do I uniquely offer? What animates me, and what do I want?"

At different stages in your life, your answers will vary. That's why each time you make a change, pause to clarify what animates you, assess your top strengths, and discern what you want to do next. Each of the five times I've changed careers, my inside journey led me to a different result—one that might not have been right at another stage of my life. Each time, I followed the rules in this book to discover what I was meant to do in that season of my life.

By discerning what you're meant to do at this stage of your career, you will:

Save time. You can focus on the most promising opportunities and dive deep to successfully land the right one rather than wasting time on scattershot applications.

Deepen your conviction. You will know why you are the right match for a specific position, and radiate the vision and confidence to demonstrate it.

Increase your ability to win. By projecting your unique relevant assets, you will stand out and inspire hiring committees to see you as the match.

People who discover joyful work are intentional and thoughtful at each time of transition. They think more about who they are and what they want to contribute, and they engage with the job market differently. The careful choices they make create a trajectory of growth and a strong foundation for career satisfaction over time.

Identifying what makes you special.

—

Rule Number 2 is about harnessing the power of self awareness to claim your unique assets and clarify your direction at each time of transition. The Milestone exercises in this chapter are designed to help you identify your differentiators and envision a job in which you will thrive. I hope you'll use the Milestone exercises to explore key dimensions of your uniqueness:

Animators: What energizes you and brings you to life.

Strengths: What you do best.

Purpose: What you feel called to do.

Your animators energize you. These are the interests, challenges, and activities that you genuinely enjoy. You thrive when your job engages your animators.

The first two Milestones will put you in touch with your animators and provide clues about what to look for in your next work adventure. Complete the Milestone exercises over a couple of days to allow space for a range of thoughts to surface. You can create an online site or use a notepad to capture your thoughts in response to these exercises.

MILESTONE
CLARIFY LIKES AND DISLIKES

This exercise provides insights that help you consider your preferred job content, culture, and context. Capture what you do and don't enjoy in your current work and life. Be expansive, and work on your dislikes as much as your likes. In each successive position, gain more of what you like and shuck or delegate the tasks you dislike.

Here are examples from my own list:

Likes
- Varied challenges, issues, and people—no two days alike.
- Ability to make things happen.
- A positive culture with diverse colleagues and ideas.
- Freedom to create my own goals and schedule.

Dislikes
- Redundant tasks—solving the same issues over and over.
- A culture that values profit at the expense of quality.
- A competitive rather than collaborative culture.
- The need to attend lots of evening events.

My actual likes and dislikes list was much longer, as yours will be. It highlighted my need to engage with a variety of challenges, issues, and people, to be constantly learning, and to set my own agenda. I like to work with a collaborative team rather than in a siloed or competitive environment. I thrive when the work is complex, varied, and growth-oriented in a culture where teamwork and quality are valued. I'm motivated by managing my priorities and time. I prize family time and should avoid jobs that require regular evening meetings, events, or calls spanning time zones.

MILESTONE
IDENTIFY YOUR ANIMATORS

To augment your list of likes and dislikes, develop a list of what brings you joy. Capture instances when you feel inspired, engaged, or energized. What was the activity, interaction, or result? What project, task, or achievement made you feel alive? When you wake up excited about the day's work, what are the highlights you anticipate? As a prompt, think back to joys from your childhood, prior jobs, or earlier life moments.

Here are some items on my "joys" list:

- Participating in a meaningful, collaborative discussion.
- Creating a high-quality solution, idea, or result.
- Analyzing and devising sustainable solutions to problems.
- Helping with career coaching, advice, or connections.
- Winning exciting new search assignments.
- Seeing family, traveling, and exercising.

Analyzing my list of joys deepened my awareness of what I wanted in my next work. It helped me see how important relationships are to me and how I derive joy by providing helpful advice, winning assignments, and growing my organization.

Together with the strengths and purpose exercises that follow, the animator exercises provide the groundwork for identifying a different and exciting new position. At each time of transition, seek out joys and challenges that animate you.

Living into your animators.

—

Joe knew it was time to make a career change from his long-time financial job. He was overdue for a spurt of professional growth and yearned for work that would engage and stretch him. He just didn't know what that should look like. He captured and analyzed his work likes and dislikes.

Joe pondered what he liked and what annoyed him in the current situation. He listed situations he found demotivating or downright unenjoyable. He enumerated his likes and dislikes, activities and interactions that gave him joy at work and at home. He enjoyed working with his team, leading new initiatives such as a recent technology implementation, analyzing financial scenario plans, and building productive relationships across the organization and with vendors.

What gave him the most joy was the time he spent volunteering for a supportive housing program that offered residents housing, coaching, career advice and training. Joe enjoyed his interactions with individuals, hearing their life stories, and helping them tackle financial and work problems. He valued collaborating with the staff and other volunteers and felt his contributions of time and money made a meaningful difference.

When Joe completed his analysis, he felt satisfied that he understood his animators. "I'm on the move to what's next," he thought. It felt good to be heading toward whatever might lie ahead.

Once you've identified your likes, dislikes, and joys, think about them in the aggregate. Dig deeper by answering these questions:

- What energizes and animates me? What stresses or bores me?
- What kinds of situations, accomplishments, or challenges make me feel alive and happy?
- What kind of culture do I thrive in?
- What everyday tasks are engaging, and what do I procrastinate on or avoid doing?
- What kind of workday environment do I most enjoy?

Are you starting to see patterns? Capture your observations.

Does more money create joy?

Study after study proves that money is important up to the point of enabling you to live the life you desire and feel secure about your future. So money matters, but only so much. Beyond that, greater compensation does not motivate more or bring greater joy. What creates joy are close relationships, alignment with values, and continual growth and learning.

Owning your strengths.

—

Every significant accomplishment you have had, and will have over time, is driven by your strengths. We do great work by leveraging our areas of strength and mitigating or minimizing our areas of weakness (we all have them!). Your combination of strengths enables you to do what no one else can do as easily or as well as you. The more your work is centered around your strengths, the more joyful and impactful it will feel.

In contrast, no one succeeds for long at work that requires them to spend time overcoming or compensating for their areas of weakness. You won't reach your potential in a situation where you're mired in areas of relative weakness.

Together with your natural areas of strength, the expertise and knowledge you have built up through education, work experience, hobbies, training, and self-improvement efforts are the key assets you offer to prospective employers.

The next couple of exercises will help you take stock of your strengths and expertise.

MILESTONE
OWN YOUR STRENGTHS

List five to eight accomplishments you've had in the last couple of years—what you have made happen that felt satisfying and made a difference. Think of accomplishments you feel proud of, whether or not others recognized them. Consider successes in your work, at home, and in other key roles you fill. Give each accomplishment a title and a sentence or two.

Once you have your list, step back. Analyze the what and

the how of these successes. For each accomplishment, ask:

- **What were the results I achieved?**
  Examples:
  - Increased revenues, awareness, reputation.
  - Built a successful, high-performing team.
  - Got my idea accepted.
  - Nailed a major presentation.
  - Won business, a promotion, a new position.

- **How did I accomplish that?**
  Examples:
  - Engaged the team, my supervisor, outside partners.
  - Listened, created a safe space, built consensus.
  - Cultivated understanding and commitment.
  - Developed and implemented a plan.
  - Studied, practiced, demonstrated good self-discipline.

- **Which strengths did I utilize to achieve these results?**
  Examples:
  - Leadership, vision, ability to project into the future.
  - Strategic, analytic, problem-solving skills.
  - Mentoring, managing, developing skills.
  - Relationship, listening, collaborative skills.
  - Communication, persuasion, logic skills.
  - Technology, detail orientation, project management skills.

Do this for each of your recent accomplishments. You will notice recurring themes and discover that your greatest accomplishments are driven by the same set of core strengths.

To analyze his strengths, Joe wrote down three main accomplishments. He listed each accomplishment, then analyzed how he achieved it. He then captured the specific strengths he utilized to achieve the accomplishment. Here are Joe's examples:

- **Stabilized and built an effective finance team.**
  How he did it:
  - Facilitated development of shared vision and goals.
  - Built trusting relationships.
  - Hired, coached, and developed good talent.
  - Built a culture of teamwork and collaboration.

  Strengths:
  - Communication.
  - Relationship skills.
  - Management.
  - Talent development.
  - Culture building.

- **Implemented a new financial technology system.**
  How he did it:
  - Convinced the executive team to make the investment.
  - Built a team around the selection and implementation process.
  - Communicated to build buy-in across the organization.
  - Stepped in to solve problems as they arose.

  Strengths:
  - Communication and persuasion skills.
  - Relationship skills.
  - Management.
  - Organizational skills.
  - Problem-solving.
  - Technical skills.

- **Streamlined systems and processes.**
  How he did it:
  - Listened to understand the problems.
  - Secured buy-in on goals and desired outcomes.
  - Communicated the benefits of streamlining.
  - Motivated a small, cross-organizational team.

  Strengths:
  - Relationship skills.
  - Strategic analytical skills.
  - Organizational skills.
  - Communication.
  - Problem-solving.
  - Management.

Several strengths turned up as drivers for every one of Joe's successes. Management skills, relationship building, communication, and problem-solving were involved in almost every success Joe had. His financial and technology skills were essential. For some of his accomplishments, he demonstrated additional skills in areas such as change management, talent development, culture building, strategic analysis, and technical know-how.

Claiming your experience.

—

Of course, employers are looking for relevant experience and particular expertise. Background and competencies are important, but your strengths and the interests that animate you are what propel your successes. I often read resumés from the bottom to trace a person's journey from their starting point to how they've navigated their careers. This provides clues to whether their next destination is a match for the position I'm hiring.

Make an inventory of your journey: fields of work, sectors, credentials, expertise, and substantive work experience. Consider expertise developed both within and beyond your work. Add any social, economic, political, cultural, equity, environmental, or other areas in which you have developed expertise.

Also consider other sectors, fields, or subjects that intrigue you. What topics have engaged your curiosity? Are there areas that deeply interest you in which you have at least some experience? Do certain community needs grab you, such as early learning or higher education, equity or religion, healthcare or climate change? Are you passionate about justice, mental health, or education? Engineering? Are you into marketing, business, or political science?

Joe listed his areas of expertise and his credentials:

- Finance: accounting, analysis, projections, management.
- Organizational skills: improving structure, processes, systems.
- Technology implementation.
- Team management and collaboration.
- Master's degree in Finance.

He captured his interests:

- Working in the context of challenges, aspirations, and growth.
- Helping people in need—generating community impact.
- Making a difference rather than just making money.

Joe noted that his core strengths are relationship-building, management, communication, organization, and problem-solving. He is good at motivating teams and building a positive culture. He thought about his areas of expertise, notably finance, organizational, technology, and management skills.

Reflecting on his animators, strengths, and areas of expertise, Joe decided to see if a nonprofit where he volunteered could utilize his financial expertise.

MILESTONE
CLAIM YOUR EXPERIENCE AND EXPERTISE

Identify your areas of expertise and interest, including the various sectors in which you have worked. Think back to what you may have learned at earlier stages of your career and education and through volunteering and outside interests.

Considering your responses, answer these questions:

- What top strengths drive my accomplishments?
- How do I create success?
- What are my expertise, knowledge, and interest areas that might suggest fields to consider for my next work?
- Which work or life experiences could provide a bridge to new areas?
- What is my unique set of strengths and abilities?

You will find it easiest to excel in roles that draw upon your strengths for as close as possible to 100 percent of the time. The surest, shortest bridge to your next work is an extension of your strengths and expertise. Remember, your strengths are transferable to different types of work. You have to help the hiring team "connect the dots" and use their imagination, but transferring our strengths to new endeavors is a critical factor in continuing to grow.

Different "best" at different stages.

Your life circumstances, capabilities, and talents evolve throughout your life and career. At each juncture, you are different, what you have to offer is different, and so are your best opportunities. That is why the inside journey is a critical first step to take at each career interval.

Discerning your purpose.

—

The term "purpose" gets tossed around frequently, but what does it really mean? I think of it this way: *Your purpose is what you are meant to be, do, or accomplish through your life and work.*

Many of us struggle to articulate our purpose. We seek to grasp it, but it can be elusive. We worry that "purpose" needs to be a grand calling, like ending hunger or reversing climate change. Those are noble causes, but far too ambitious for any one person. Discerning your purpose, at least in a general way, helps ground and guide you. Your purpose provides a kind of North Star and shows you the direction you should keep heading.

Your purpose will evolve throughout your stages of life. The parent of a young child with developmental challenges may define his or her purpose as ensuring the child's safety and well-being. At a later juncture in life, when the child has grown and achieved greater independence, that same parent's purpose could be to enhance the family's finances through a stable work situation or to take on stimulating new work.

Your purpose is what you are meant to be, do, or accomplish through your life and work.

Your purpose can be as simple as "taking care of those close to me." It can be a sense of calling, such as "making a difference in the lives of children" through a particular mission, faith, or charitable endeavor. It can be as ambitious as "building a growing, sustainable enterprise that employs thousands of people and supports their families with health care and living wages."

Stephen Covey said, "Begin with the end in mind." At each interval of change, stop to analyze where you are, to think forward about your life, and to revisit your purpose.

MILESTONE
DISCERN YOUR PURPOSE

First, consider what matters to you at this stage of your life by reflecting upon each of these questions:

- What do I care about? What matters most now?
- What would I like to make happen in the near future?
- What difference do I want to make?

Then, projecting forward:

- What do I want to accomplish during my lifetime?
- What kind of legacy do I want to create?
- What do I want people to say about me at my funeral?

And finally, consider this question to create a statement of purpose.

- What am I on this planet to do?

Take into account what makes sense at your current stage of life. What, if anything, should be deferred to a later stage? You can accomplish many different things—but not all at the same time. Capture your draft purpose on the sheet with your animators and strengths.

Here's how Joe reflected on his animators, strengths, and purpose.

Animators
Likes: Relationships, collaboration, helping others.
Dislikes: Environment lacking aspiration and growth.
Joys: Making a difference for others who are less fortunate.

Strengths and expertise
Strengths: Leadership, relationship building, management, communication, problem-solving .
Expertise: Finance, operations, technology.

Purpose
Helping people in need find their way to better life circumstances.

Joe asked himself: Where does my gladness (animators, strengths, purpose) meet the world's hunger (work opportunities)?

He wondered what kind of position would suit him best. Could he earn an income doing it? What would that look like? Putting all this together, Joe envisioned a leadership role utilizing his finance and management skills, most likely in a nonprofit organization.

Envisioning your next destination.

—

Congratulations! You have completed important, hard "inside" work. Hopefully, it has been enjoyable and illuminating. You now have a deeper sense of the kind of work you are best suited to do, as well as some essential guidance for your next step. But how does this knowledge connect with your actual opportunities in today's actual job market?

Factoring in the results of your inside journey, develop what I call your "buckets of opportunity." These are directions you see as reasonable possibilities for you, given your animators, strengths, and purpose. Each of your buckets represents a position, organization, or work situation that could feel right for you.

To identify possible directions, start by considering contexts in which your animators, strengths, and purpose might be valued. These can be somewhat broad, not necessarily role-specific. They should be directions that offer promise, hypotheses about where you could find your best match. Identifying these gives you a solid starting point for your job-seeking tasks.

*Where does my gladness meet
the world's hunger?*

Joe identified three buckets. He realized that every organizational culture and situation is different, so he would have to discern, through interviews and research, which opportunities within those buckets would actually be a fit.

He knew his ultimate match would depend upon factors including culture, compensation, and day-to-day work assignments. Here are the buckets of opportunity Joe identified:

Operational role in a nonprofit organization	Financial management in a business with social purpose	Financial leadership in a nonprofit organization

Looking at his three buckets, Joe felt most drawn to a nonprofit operational or financial role. But he was also confident that a company with a strong social purpose could fit, given his corporate background. He narrowed his search to local organizations, realizing this was not the time in his life to relocate as his children were still in school. His next step was deciding on an effective way to explore these opportunities, which is the topic of the next chapter.

MILESTONE
FOCUS ON YOUR BUCKETS OF OPPORTUNITY

Now, discover and capture your buckets. Find the themes in your animators, strengths, purposes, and experience. Where and in what kinds of positions might you and your abilities be highly valued?

Finding the right match: Kathy's story

Over the course of my five careers, each change I made moved me closer to a 100 percent match with my animators, strengths, and purpose. In these moves, I also sought to minimize the time spent on my dislikes and weaknesses.

In my role as SVP of external relations at CARE, the global relief and development organization, I was responsible for private fundraising, branding, and marketing. I managed a team of 125 at headquarters and across a dozen satellite offices. Extensive domestic and international travel was a material aspect of the work—at a time when I had two sons in elementary school. I loved the work, but 60-hour work weeks and travel took their toll on my family.

Seven years into my CARE position, one son reached his eighth birthday, and the other became a teenager. I realized it was time to seek a job with less pressure and travel. I gave the organization several months' notice so I could openly seek my next opportunity while still working. Because it's harder to find work when you're out of a job, it's best to avoid leaving until you know where you're landing.

Avoid leaving until you know where you're landing.

Finding a next career adventure while still working full-time requires extra effort. In my case, I woke earlier than usual and carved out time in the early mornings and on weekends. I gave myself daily assignments in order to assess my animators, strengths, and purpose. I asked myself questions to clarify my sense of what could be next. Here is what I discovered:

Animators

From my likes, dislikes, and joys, I characterized the kind of work environment that energizes me:

Likes: Teamwork, innovation, achieving positive results.

Dislikes: Bureaucracy, micromanagement, stagnation.

Joys: Making things happen, and making a difference.

Strengths and expertise

I analyzed what I do best by listing out accomplishments and experiences.

Strengths: Bringing people together around vision and collaboration, inspiring people to be their best, writing, planning, accomplishing goals.

Expertise: Fundraising, marketing, communication, client service, advertising, public relations, international development.

Purpose

I reflected on my purpose at this particular stage of my life. It was "Making a difference in other people's lives while being more available as a parent."

Buckets of opportunity

My three buckets came into view, and I was ready to move forward in my search:

Nonprofit executive management	Marketing leadership in a company with social mission	Leadership in a mission-oriented communications firm

Deciding if you should stay put.

—

Even if you're ready for change, making a move might not be the best solution at this time in your career. Staying put at the current organization could be a wise decision if you've only been there for a year or two; if there's a possibility of new responsibilities; or if the effort of changing jobs would add excessive stress.

Staying put turned out to be the best option for Trina:

As Trina worked to discern her animators, strengths, and purpose, she realized her company was actually the right place for her now. While she felt stalled in her current position and had no immediate promotion opportunities, she felt good overall about the company's values and products. Her learning curve had flattened, and much of her job felt routine. "If I'm not growing, I'm falling behind," she worried.

Rather than leave, Trina decided to create her own new growth trajectory. She sought advice from a trusted colleague and eventually her manager. She worked her way to stretch assignments that challenged her and made her more visible in the organization. She requested and received leadership coaching. Eventually, she was able to add new responsibilities and move to a more senior role in the organization with a larger team.

Having reimagined her work, Trina happily stayed for two more years, then began the journey for her next adventure.

New life begins beyond your comfort zone.

It's been said that the two most important days of your life are the day you are born and the day you know why. I want you to unlock your "why" and find the joy of working in the career you were made for. The more your career attends to your animators, strengths, and purpose, the more intentional you can be about finding a sweet-spot match where you can do work that matters to you. People whose work aligns with their passion experience a special level of joy.

When you have clarity on your animators, strengths, purpose, and buckets of opportunity, it's time to move to the next stage of your search.

Rule Number 1 revealed the importance of a forward looking mindset focused on *going to* rather than *coming from*.

Rule Number 2 is about deepening your knowledge of your unique assets and discerning potential work destinations.

Rule Number 3 will stress the value of connecting with people to connect with opportunity.

Remember that taking a big leap is often what you are meant to do and what will accelerate your career and your joy at work. If you're not growing, you are falling behind. Be courageous and ambitious! New life begins beyond your comfort zone.

Here are three bonus questions:

- What next job would be bold and build on my strengths and experience?

- What am I "best in the world" at?

- What might be holding me back?

TOP TAKEAWAYS

- Take an "inside journey" before you start your job search.

- Clarify what animates you and your strengths, expertise, and life purpose.

- Define your buckets of opportunity: sectors, types of positions, and places to investigate as you undertake your search.

Connect with People

Congratulations on starting your search by exploring what animates you, your strengths, and your purpose (Rule Number 2). Knowing your buckets of opportunity prepares you to target sectors and roles for which you are well suited and to find people to help you along the way. Self-awareness prepares you to assess the opportunities that come your way, to present yourself as a unique fit, and ultimately to win the job you're meant to have.

The secret to finding great work is people. The odds are that you will land your next job through someone you know, have known, or will meet in the course of your search. I'm not talking about generic "networking," which can be unfocused and transactional. Instead, focus on building authentic relationships. Connecting with people in and adjacent to your buckets of opportunity will accelerate your journey and help distinguish you from a sea of applicants.

People accelerate your journey.

Reaching your destination through people.

—

Relationships that are authentic, not just transactional, are invaluable to your search. By connecting with a broad and growing set of people, you will:

- Gain insider advice about new fields and positions of interest.
- Discover insights about yourself and how others see your talents.
- Learn about, and access, opportunities you would not otherwise hear about.
- Benefit from extra consideration, such as an interview or a second look.

Referrals can get you in the door, but they don't guarantee an offer. That's up to you. Rules Number 4 and Number 5 reveal the secrets on how to optimize your resumé and prevail in a job search.

You may be thinking you don't currently know people related to your buckets of opportunity. Or perhaps you worry that your network is too small. You may already have begun reaching out to your circles and connected with an initial handful of people. You may feel you've already tapped your existing connections and wonder where to go from here.

First, take heart: You'll be surprised at how many people you actually know, have known, or can get to know. You almost certainly have not exhausted your current connections, and you will be able to identify more people to help accelerate your search.

---

*You'll be surprised at how
many people you know or can reach.*

Start by thinking about the places you've lived, the schools you've attended, the religious and community organizations you've belonged to, paid and volunteer roles you've held over the years. Now, begin to list the people you know from those experiences, noting those who may have knowledge or connections in and around your buckets of opportunity.

Even if you've been out of touch for years, former colleagues, classmates, and acquaintances are almost always pleased to reconnect, and almost everyone, given the chance, would like to help. For your list, consider:

- People you have worked with, including current teammates you can talk with confidentially.
- Your earlier jobs. Remember colleagues, partners, and clients you've worked with. Where are they now? Might any of them be working in your areas of interest?
- Former classmates, professors, and teachers.
- People you know through volunteering, civic groups,

hobbies, religious groups, sports, and other activities.

- Members of your professional community and adjacent communities.

- Neighbors and acquaintances you run into while walking the dog, shopping, dropping children at school, etc.

- Friends, relatives, associates, acquaintances, and anyone they can introduce you to.

Most people would like to be helpful if they can.

Consider new people you could connect with or seek an introduction to, or reasonably reach, including:

- Connections through academic or alumni associations.

- Recruiters conducting searches that fall in your bucket areas.

- Associates and connections of family members and friends.

- People in organizations you might be targeting.

Develop a good long list—at least fifty names if you can—and keep adding to it. Adding relevant names from LinkedIn and suggestions from your current circle of acquaintances, you can generate a robust roster. You may want to put the names in a database to track outreach, referrals, and follow-ups. Here is a basic template for a spreadsheet or database. It will serve you well, during and following your search:

CONTACT DATABASE RUBRIC

Contact	Occupation/ Location	Introduced by	Comments
Joan Smith email/phone	VP Sales, ABC Company	John Adams email/phone	Left voicemail message
Barbara Jones email/phone	Director of Marketing, XYZ Firm	Joan Smith email/phone	Contacted: 2/24 Meeting: 3/10

The people you identify, connect with, or meet along the way can accelerate your search. Approach each of them in a way that is authentic and relational. You will find that most people like to be helpful if they can. Make it easy for them to help. Express interest in them, ask for advice, and demonstrate curiosity.

Taking charge by activating relationships.

—

Taking the initiative to cultivate current and new relationships will pay off in various ways, in both the short term and the long run. Your contacts offer insights into yourself and the areas of opportunity you're exploring. They can help you identify and move toward strong opportunities—or avoid negative situations. The degree to which you take charge of this part of your search and proactively create a resource network will impact your success.

Remember Selena, who was dealing with a values mismatch?

Selena was working in marketing for a fossil fuel company, and her values were not aligned with the organization's business. She had joined the company a few years back, before becoming acutely aware of the realities of climate change and the impact of fossil fuels. She had earned promotions and increased compensation, yet she had developed gnawing concerns about the harm the company's business had on the climate and on people living in low-income neighborhoods near power plants.

Approach everyone in a way that is authentic and relational.

Although her company was advancing a renewable energy strategy, that was a much lower priority than the main business. Selena believed in the promise of renewable energy and tried, unsuccessfully, to move to that part of the company. Those opportunities were rarely available.

Selena didn't think she knew anyone who could help her navigate toward a job in the field of renewable energy. She was unsure what it would take to break into a new sector. She felt she would be better aligned with an organization fighting for clean energy and the environment, but worried that nonprofits pay less than corporate jobs. "How can I find my way to work that aligns with my purpose and pays well?" she wondered.

Selena's strengths were in communications, marketing, and project management. She had some knowledge, and considerable passion, about solar and other clean-energy solutions. She was drawn both to the field of clean energy and to nonprofit work in poverty alleviation. She had a special interest in helping children in low-income neighborhoods and had been volunteering for a community-based nonprofit on weekends.

These strengths and interests led her to three buckets of opportunity:

A marketing position in a clean energy company or a nonprofit	A communication, marketing or project role in an environmental organization	A role in a company with authentic commitment to social issues

Selena knew her next step was finding people to talk with who could point her in the direction of relevant opportunities and potentially introduce her.

Finding helpful people.

—

You can open doors through people in your past, current, or emerging network. To maximize your time, focus on people whose work or background relates to your buckets of opportunity. Connecting with people has never been easier. You can reach almost anyone through LinkedIn, Facebook, Instagram, and other social media. You don't need to know their contact information. Making initial contact virtually is fast and efficient.

Your LinkedIn profile is where recruiters—and everyone else—turn for an overview of your background. I'm always surprised at how many people neglect to curate and add to their profiles. Like a company's website, this is your all-purpose brand identity and a window into your expertise. Spend time updating LinkedIn to ensure it reflects positively and communicates your background effectively.

Your LinkedIn profile is your brand identity.

LinkedIn is the "professional networking capitol." Growing contacts there is easy and important. Selectively accept invitations that are suggested for you. LinkedIn will push you possible contacts. Accept by clicking "Connect" to invite them. Search for others, including the contacts of your contacts. You can invite as many as you want. You can join groups to extend your presence. Post regularly to magnify your numbers, attract likes, and engage new contacts.

Maintain and increase your connections. They are a searchable, invaluable resource for connecting and communicating, especially during a search. Employers care that you are connected in your industry. During a discussion of a possible candidate, for example, my client looked up a name on LinkedIn. "He has fewer than 500 contacts," she observed. That candidate was dropped.

Selena, who wanted to find a better match with her values than the business of her employer, developed a strategic list of first contacts and began to reach out selectively. Here are examples of Selena's email and LinkedIn subject lines:

- Request for your advice on the clean energy sector
- Advice on the solar energy sector, sent by . . . (name)
- With thanks, requesting a short call

Once you connect via LinkedIn or social media, be tenacious about turning connections into live contacts and conversations.

> Selena was able to locate thirty individuals and message them on LinkedIn. In her messages, she asked whether they'd be willing to give her advice. A couple of people responded the same day. She asked whether they'd be willing to have a short call, and she was able to send calendar invitations to secure appointments. Others took more time, but a number of people responded and offered to help.
>
> For the busiest people and those without any close connections to her, Selena sent second, and sometimes third, messages to prompt their response. Whenever someone had referred her, she was sure to mention the connection, which increased the speed and rate of responses.

Making contact with some people requires persistence, but most of the time, your patience and tenacity will be rewarded with receptivity. These connections often lead to positive interactions that feel good. They often lead to helpful advice, referrals, and personal introductions.

We often hesitate to reach out to people we've lost contact with. We don't remember how we lost contact and might worry about an awkward reception. The pleasant surprise is that most people are glad to reconnect or even to connect for the first time.

Asking for the right thing.

—

Connect with people by asking for their advice. It's easy for most people to agree to sharing their expertise. On the other hand, if you ask someone about open jobs they know about, you may hit a dead end. They may not know of any that would be relevant. Besides, that question is transactional—can you help me get a job?—rather than relationship building.

Connect with people by asking for their advice.

The way you approach people makes a difference. If you enter the conversation with curiosity about their work or a desire to connect, you are cultivating a relationship. If you already have a connection, provide an update on your activities and ask for their advice as you consider new career opportunities. You will benefit from their insights and potential introductions.

It can take monumental perseverance to schedule a call or secure a meeting. Don't let that discourage you. People are busy with their priorities. If you are polite and patient, the majority will talk with you. Through your positive interaction, you are initiating a new source of information, connection, and potential help. Meeting in person is ideal, but virtual meetings can also be powerful. Sometimes a simple phone call is the only option. Be patient and remain committed to meeting the people who can help you along your journey, even if they don't respond for some time.

The more people you meet in and around your buckets of opportunity, the better your chances of discovering opportunities.

By becoming top of mind and staying in contact, you multiply your chances of relevant referrals. Your network will be rooting for you to wind up in a great place.

Through all of your interactions, keep a mindset of openness and optimism. Envision yourself as exploring work possibilities rather than as a job seeker.

Your network will be rooting for you
to wind up in a great place.

Making your contact list.

—

You may start slowly, jotting down some obvious contacts. If you are in a position where confidentiality is paramount, your first tranche of names must be people you can trust to maintain confidentiality. When you're ready to begin a full search, push yourself to generate a list of fifty or more initial contacts. That way, when you fully activate your search, you generate progress from the outset. Where to begin?

Selena was initially stumped and overwhelmed. Then she remembered that her cousin Jan used to work for an environmental nonprofit and might be willing to introduce her to someone in that organization. She recalled that Paul, who went to her church, worked at a nonprofit. She felt she could probably talk confidentially with Mike, who was leading clean energy initiatives for her company. She began to write those names down, then added a former science professor who she knew had consulted with the solar industry. A couple more names came to mind.

When she researched the nonprofit sector in her area, she discovered organizations and positions she didn't expect, titles relevant to her background, as well as posted openings. In some cases, job descriptions and the names of hiring managers were included. She captured those names as well.

She then went on LinkedIn and found that her network included a few other individuals who were working in clean energy. LinkedIn also pushed names to her of people she might want to connect with, some of them relevant to her buckets of opportunity.

With a little effort, Selena was preparing to make her way into the worlds of clean energy and nonprofit organizations. She was navigating with intention and taking charge. It was exciting and intimidating. And hopeful.

Discovering a new trajectory.

—

When I was seeking my next career adventure after a decade of work in advertising, I wasn't sure what my buckets of opportunity were. I'd identified what makes me joyful, including volunteering and nonprofit work. My strengths included marketing, strategy, writing, and developing shared vision. I knew I wanted to move in those general directions. I was open to a broad range of possibilities.

One of the people I reached out to was someone I'd known at my advertising agency. Ann had been a role model and a mentor to me. Having moved on to bigger things in her career, she was nevertheless happy to advise me. We had worked together on a public service campaign, so she knew I was a committed volunteer. I shared my reflections on possible directions and asked for her advice.

People make the difference between finding a good opportunity and missing out.

A couple of weeks later, Ann called to let me know about a position a nonprofit board she served on—CARE—had just announced. They were getting ready to search for a new SVP of fundraising and marketing. I knew about the organization and admired the mission.

Ann told me to call the recruiter at their search firm. I wasn't at all sure I was a match. "I know marketing, but I don't know fundraising," I argued. "Just call," she said.

Finding work in a new city.

—

While corporate relocations are less common now, many people move to a new city and have to start over. Doing that successfully includes building upon the foundation you've established in your prior location and developing a whole new network. It requires patience and strategy. Here's how Gwen approached her move:

Gwen's husband John was recruited to the job of his dreams. She wanted to support him, but the position was based in another city where she had no connections. Besides, they had finally found a school where their son was thriving, and she didn't want to disrupt him.

The couple made an agonizing decision: John would accept the job, and they could live in separate cities until their son finished the school year and Gwen found work. To begin her search in the new city, Gwen set out to build a network in the new location. She was fortunate to start with introductions from her husband's new associates.

Going in warm.

—

If you have applied online, you have experienced the sensation of pitching your resumé into a black hole. On rare occasions you may get a response along the lines of "we'll get back to you." Sometimes postings are for phantom jobs, crafted to attract applicants who might fill other less-attractive positions. Applicant tracking systems (ATS) will screen out most unsolicited resumés, and overwhelmed HR staff usually lack the bandwidth to consider or respond to them. Rarely does an electronic application turn into a real opportunity.

When you decide to pursue an opportunity, try to connect with someone in or close to the organization so your starting point is "warm." This will help distinguish you from others who are competing for the position. You won't always identify a connection, but it's well worth trying. Before you apply for any job, scour your current and potential contacts for someone who can introduce you.

If you don't have a current way in, try to identify the hiring manager or recruiter. If you're certain you're a strong fit for the position and your background matches the main mandate, try contacting the hiring manager or headhunter directly.

I've received many such "cold" calls.

A decade ago, Jane left me a voicemail: "I am a good match for the director position you're hiring for at ABC Company. May we talk?" Because I'm seeking the right match, I respond to calls from individuals who say they have the expertise. In many cases, the caller turns out not to be a good fit. Every now and then they are a real contender, which is why I pay attention to these calls.

Jane followed up with her resumé and was in fact a strong candidate, with relevant credentials and experience. She had excellent interpersonal and team management skills. She won the job. Ten years later, Jane is still at that organization, having been promoted a couple of times, and she still loves her work.

As a headhunter, I interact with hundreds of people, including many who just don't match the needs of a particular position. It can have to do with specific experience, alignment with the organization's direction, or fit with their culture. I respect each individual's talents and abilities, whether or not they fit the position at hand. Each talented person I meet, whether right for the immediate opening or not, becomes part of our search firm database and a potential future candidate. In the quest to find the just-right match, I want to talk with any individual who might become the hire for this or a future opportunity.

Avoid time-wasting applications
- Don't pursue a job unless it's truly a match for your strengths and experience.
- Avoid applying cold and online.
- Avoid sending your resumé "cold." Seek a warm introduction or invitation.
- Don't bother with scatter-shot applications. Target opportunities you're uniquely suited for.
- Don't submit a generic application. Tailor your submission to the specific opportunity.

Relying on contacts.

—

When you're looking for your first job, putting together a list of contacts may seem especially daunting. What's more, many of us avoid contacting people our relatives or teachers suggest. Leveraging such connections may feel like bringing others into parts of our life we'd rather keep private. We may worry about using contacts to gain unearned or unfair advantage. Asking people you don't know for advice can feel awkward or like an imposition. Do it anyway.

While we may have reasons to avoid asking advice from those closest to us, their help can make the difference between finding a good opportunity and missing out. Remember Gordon?

Gordon graduated from college during the recession of 2008. Unemployment was high and entry-level jobs scarce. I suggested he start reaching out to his family, teachers, and others to build a network around his search. With a liberal arts degree in music, Gordon hoped to find an entry-level position in the arts, a highly competitive field. I gave him a couple of people to contact and promised to think of more.

A warm introduction elevated his resumé from one in a stack to the handful that received a closer look.

He balked at my suggestion to start reaching out. "I'm an introvert," he protested. He felt uneasy about reaching out to virtual strangers, and he resisted the suggestion to access new opportunities by leveraging other people's relationships. He procrastinated.

His first calls were painful, yet he realized that submitting applications online was getting him nowhere. Despite putting effort into those applications, he never heard back from most employers. He finally began contacting the handful of people recommended by teachers and family. He was surprised to receive a growing number of positive responses.

Some people just gave him advice and encouragement. Others took the time to provide referrals. Several pointed Gordon toward organizations that were hiring. It was a warm introduction to one arts organization that elevated Gordon's resumé from one among hundreds to the handful that received a closer look.

MILESTONE
CONNECT TO ACCELERATE YOUR SEARCH

Think about your buckets of opportunity. In what kinds of organizations, professions, or sectors might you find those opportunities? What kinds of connections could you make to learn about those areas, to meet people working in them, and to seek referrals to open positions? Make your list.

Valuing people as your sustainable advantage.

—

Over the course of a successful search, people you meet will impart advice and referrals. Many will become part of your on-going network, leading to future opportunities. If you cultivate these relationships and help other people with their journeys, you will develop a network for life.

The term "networking" is overused and often reduced to a purely transactional purpose that doesn't center relationship building. As a life practice, cultivating a network of individuals as friends, advisors, and referral sources is essential. My career experience, and that of people I coach, proves that it is people who make the difference in accelerating your career and helping you find and win joyful work.

This is especially true for people making a transition to a new city or industry.

I have had the experience of building a network out of scratch. My family relocated to Atlanta and left New York, where we had lived for decades, for my SVP job at CARE. A few years later, my children needed more attention and I had to face the fact that my high-travel, 60-hour-a-week position was causing harm to our family. I needed to find work in our new hometown to devote more time to our young sons as they navigated elementary and middle school. I struggled to address several interrelated dilemmas:

- I had no network in Atlanta. CARE is global and I had extensive travel, so almost everyone I knew in my new city was a work colleague.

- The visibility of my role made cultivating new relationships risky; and my time was constrained by a demanding schedule and small children at home.

- If I departed without giving several months' notice, it could harm the organization and my relationships with colleagues.

To make space for a job search, I took a risk: I resigned, with six months' notice. I gave CARE notice in June and worked as promised through December. That provided time for the organization to recruit my replacement and for me to make a smooth transition.

It was a gamble. I was betting that conducting an intensive, transparent search would enable me to turn up opportunities and find my next work adventure. By being transparent, I was able to leverage relationships within CARE while developing an all-new network in Atlanta. Being open meant I would not have to hide or limit my job-hunting activities.

Following the roadmap in this book, here's the journey I took:

- I identified my animators, strengths, and purpose. To do that, I woke up 30-45 minutes earlier each day to capture my thoughts in a journal I started just for my search.
- I developed buckets of opportunity and a plan with a timeline. As I considered what my next adventure might be, I consulted a handful of trusted advisors, seeking their advice about my next move.
- I developed a list of people to contact, including members of the CARE team, beginning with an initial handful of names.

Being open meant I would not have to hide job-hunting activities.

I gave notice to CARE in June, promising to work through that year. The goal statement I developed for my search plan was: "I will start an exciting new job in January." That gave me six months to create a network out of scratch and to identify and compete for opportunities I determined to be a good match. My database of contacts started with fifteen names. Over the course of the next few months, the list grew tenfold to over 150 names.

Thanks to the people in my growing network, I had developed several potential opportunities by October, and by mid-November, I had decided on my next work adventure: leading the communications firm Porter Novelli in Atlanta. I worked through that year at CARE, as promised, and moved in January to my next adventure. Thanks to the contacts database I had created, I was able to thank everyone who helped along the way and to stay in touch after beginning at Porter Novelli.

A number of the people I met during that search became clients or introduced potential clients in the first months of my new job. Many remain friends to this day. One of the people I met during that search later founded BoardWalk Consulting, and, several years later, recruited me to the firm. Both the job at Porter Novelli and my current position as a headhunter at BoardWalk have been perfect fits for these stages of my life.

Creating your plan.

—

The time it will take you to secure your next position will depend on several factors:

- How much you're able to focus and follow through to connect with people and opportunities; and your creativity and tenacity.
- The degree of alignment between your actual experience and the role you are seeking.
- The seniority of the role you're seeking.

In general, the more senior the hire, the longer the search will take. Expect a quicker search if your background, knowledge, and experience are close matches for the position you seek. Conversely, if you are switching sectors or looking for something quite different from your work experience, the competition will be tougher and your search will likely take longer. No matter where you're going, though, people will help get you there.

Working from a plan helps ensure that you reach your destination. As you embark on the journey, set your goal and milestones: "By x date, I will have a joyful new position."

Set and hit ambitious milestones.

It pays to create a simple plan that's informed by your desired destination and when you want to arrive. Make your plan ambitious but achievable, with dates and milestones. If possible, narrow down your aspiration: "By **x** date, I will be working in **y** kind of position." Work back from your desired date of arrival to design the progression of your plan.

Assign yourself goals and milestones, for example:

- Reach out to five people/day.
- Meet with at least two people a week.
- Attend at least four events/month.
- By the end of September, talk with 30+ people and have at least three live interviews.
- In January, begin a new job.

Hold yourself to the plan. Ideally, work with an accountability partner, such as your spouse, a trusted colleague, or a close friend. Check in regularly with your partner to stay on track and to make course corrections as needed. The partner is a sounding board to talk through opportunities as they emerge.

The discipline of a realistic plan helps ensure on-time, right-place arrival.

Unfortunately, most people undertake a search without a plan. Without intentionality, a plan, and milestones, you can drift, month after month and year after year, without discovering a great next opportunity. The discipline of a realistic plan and timeline helps ensure on-time, right-place arrival. Your plan will transition you from where you are now to where you want to be.

MILESTONE
DEVISE A GAME PLAN

A plan turns your aspiration into reality. Develop a game plan for your transition. Here is a sample plan that begins with an end-goal: "I will start a great new job in x month/year." Once you set the destination, design the steps and timetable to guide your progress.

SEARCH PLAN RUBRIC

Topic	Actions	Timing+Metrics	Progress
Connect through people	• Build a list of people in and around my buckets • Research openings, websites, and people at organizations of interest • Add to database	By X date: 30 contacts By Y date: 50+ contacts	
Ask for advice	• Connect, meet, ask for advice and referrals • Follow up, send thanks • Add new names	First 20 calls/ meetings by X date Next 20 by Y date	
Focus on key opportunities	• Understand the bullseye • Generate introductions • Customize resumé and interactions • Prepare for meetings: connect the dots	X initial calls/ interviews by Y date	
Stand out to win	• Focus on the most promising opportunities • Give examples, follow up, go beyond • Reject an offer until you're sure it's a match	2-3 promising opportunities by Y date X kind of offer by Y date	
Transition	• Prepare for transition • Orchestrate a timely, gracious departure • Take some time off • Develop your entry strategy plan		

TOP TAKEAWAYS

Relationships that are real and reciprocal are your sustainable advantage across the arc of your career and life.

- The secret to finding work you love is connecting with people.
- Finding and connecting with people is easier than ever.
- Most people are happy to help.
- Ask for advice, not a job.
- Make a plan: by x date, I will have a joyful new job.

Focus on the Bullseye

In the pool of applicants for any job, the vast majority will come in second. For any good opening, there's no shortage of talented, qualified individuals with relevant experience. In-demand jobs attract hundreds of applicants. The hiring committee will vet a small number of candidates, and fewer than ten are likely to make it through rounds of interviews. Only one candidate will receive an offer. I want that candidate to be you.

Start by being selective about how you spend your time in a job search. Applying itself is easy, but securing the offer requires substantial effort. If you don't feel passionate about the job or if you doubt you'll stand out in a competitive candidate pool, save your efforts for a different search where you're more likely to prevail.

Only one candidate will get the offer.
I want that candidate to be you.

Don't apply to lots of positions. Focus on just the opportunities you believe could be a great fit. Only seek roles that are a genuinely strong match, and tailor your resumé to the specifications and bullseye. Present your background and experience *in light of the position requirements.* Once you're confident about an opportunity, lean in. Pour yourself into winning.

Discovering the job's bullseye.

Hiding within every job description is the "bullseye"—the central mandate the hired individual must address. Often, the mandate is obscured by a laundry list of responsibilities, skills, and mandatory qualifications. Position descriptions can be exhaustive—and exhausting! Whether or not the description is clear, try to discern the central issue, need, or problem that is driving the search.

Members of the hiring team usually have an intuitive sense of what matters most, but they may not have explicit understanding or alignment about the bullseye. Often the focus and aspirations for a position are clarified over the course of the search process. Every job has multiple facets, of course, but there is almost always a critical mandate. The successful candidate will tease out that bullseye and demonstrate how they will deliver on that. So your challenge is to read between the lines!

Aiming to hit the bullseye.

—

You will find the bullseye at the intersection of the position itself and a major organizational challenge. The opening may have been caused by someone's departure. It may be a newly-created role in response to a need of the organization. Knowing that can help you understand the main mandate. To discern the bullseye, consider: What's keeping management awake at night? What is the key accomplishment the organization needs the individual in this position to achieve?

Here are some examples of bullseyes:

- To grow revenues.
- To increase or diversify new business.
- To create infrastructure or capacity.
- To lead an important strategic change or a new direction.
- To build the organization's visibility or reputation.
- To galvanize the team to perform better.
- To lead transformation.
- To reorganize or downsize.
- To recruit, develop, and retain talent.

Tease out the bullseye and demonstrate your ability to deliver on it.

The position description for a sales manager includes responsibilities such as motivating the team, providing excellent client service, and knowing the products. But the bullseye is *increasing sales.* Product knowledge and relevant industry experience can factor in, together with other assets like organization and ability to travel. These are among the invisible boxes the hiring committee wants to check.

Because the bullseye is growing sales, your resumé, cover letter, and success examples should first and foremost address your track record of increasing sales.

Understanding the larger context.

—

Once you've identified the bullseye, gauge the match with your own animators, strengths, and experience. Learn what you can about the context of the opportunity, the current business situation, and the culture. Is this an organization with a long track record or more of a startup? Is this particular industry booming, stagnant, or declining? Is the sales cycle for their offerings short and urgent or long and complex? What does the base of current or potential customers look like? What is the culture of the organization? What's their DNA? More insight empowers you to move forward (or not) with greater clarity.

Consider how differently the same job specifications might translate in different organizational contexts, calling for different abilities:

- An organization that is growing rapidly versus one that is facing a slowdown, potential layoffs, or acquisition.

- A company that is changing its strategy, about to merge, or seeking to enter new markets versus an organization that's stable and possibly less ambitious.

- An entrepreneurial culture that thrives on innovation, versus one with longstanding approaches.

Do your homework. Search the organization's website and social media. Find someone who can provide insight into the organization. Discovering the bullseye and the specific context helps you position yourself.

Differentiating the bullseye in similar job descriptions.

—

Michelle wanted to apply her financial skills to a position that was consistent with her experience and values. For finance and other roles with established boilerplate skill sets, the list of responsibilities is similar regardless of the organization's unique context.

What's keeping management awake at night?

The following description could work for many different businesses. It could work for a company that's in fast-paced, high-growth mode or one that's declining and needs to stabilize. It could be relevant to a company managing a reputational challenge or a well-regarded nonprofit. When basic responsibilities are boilerplate, the description is just the start of what you need to know in order to prevail as a candidate.

Here's the position description that was provided to Michelle:

FINANCE DIRECTOR

Building for a Healthy Future (BHF)

—

About Us: BHF is dedicated to environmentally sustainable built solutions. We are seeking a dynamic Finance Director to join our team and contribute to the financial success and strategic growth of our organization.

Responsibilities:

1. Financial Planning and Strategy
- Develop and implement financial strategies aligned with the company's objectives.
- Drive financial planning, budgeting, and forecasting processes.

2. Financial Management
- Oversee the preparation of accurate and timely financial reports.
- Ensure compliance with accounting principles, standards, and regulations.
- Identify, assess financial risks, implementing risk management.
- Monitor and manage liquidity and cash flow.

3. Corporate Finance
- Lead mergers, acquisitions, strategic financial initiatives.
- Evaluate investment opportunities.

4. Financial Analysis
- Conduct in-depth financial analysis to support decision-making.
- Provide insights into financial trends and performance.

5. Team Leadership
- Lead and mentor finance team, fostering a culture of excellence.
- Develop and implement training programs for finance staff.

Michelle realized these functions could apply to companies or nonprofits of various sizes with very different circumstances and needs. Because she had to overcome the disadvantage of her four-year career gap, she knew she had to identify a strong match with her prior experience to have a fighting chance. She worked on figuring out the bullseye and learning more about the organization and its challenges. She wanted to make sure the opportunity aligned with her strengths. Michelle knew the mandate of the finance role could vary widely with possibilities that could include:

- The goal to expedite growth through acquisitions and investments.

  Bullseye: Proven expertise in a competitive, fast-paced industry.

- Rebuilding after downsizing and staff departures.

  Bullseye: Agile management, communication, and team leadership skills; experience helping an organization stabilize and move forward.

- Recovering from a data breach or other setback and preparing to rebuild business and reputation.

  Bullseye: strategic risk, problem solving, and crisis management.

- Building systems to manage diversified funding sources, partners, and affiliates.

  Bullseye: complex, multi-site financial, and operational expertise.

While all organizations require strong financial skills, the bullseye for their specific finance roles can differ wildly. In a successful candidate, they could be looking for:

- Background in a high-growth environment.
- An outstanding manager, communicator, and culture builder.
- Experience managing crises and mitigating risks.
- Complex multi-site, multi-revenue stream, global experience.

Michelle's last organization was a high-growth engineering firm where she had thrived. She could secure glowing references relevant to that kind of environment. She was animated by team building, fast-paced decision-making, and growth.

Research the organization online and through people.

Based on BHF's online presence, the company appeared ambitious and focused on high growth. It was environmentally conscious—the kind of business approach Michelle felt she would enjoy. In search of more information or an introduction to the company, she scrolled through her LinkedIn and email connections.

Michelle couldn't find a connection to anyone related to the organization. She reached out to several people in the sector. Eventually, she was introduced to someone in a different department of BHF. After email and LinkedIn outreach, Michelle was able to secure a phone call that helped her learn more about the organization. After that positive conversation, Michelle asked whether the individual might feel comfortable forwarding her resumé to the hiring manager. Her new BHF connection agreed to forward Michelle's resumé to the hiring manager. This increased Michelle's chances of getting noticed and considered.

If you are interested in a specific opportunity, do your homework. Research the organization online and through people you know. Ask questions to learn as much as you can. Deepen your knowledge about the organization and the position description so you can discern the bullseye and other key requirements.

Based on your research, make your determination:

- Am I a strong potential candidate for this position?
- Do I sense potential alignment with the organization?
- Does the bullseye align with my animators, strengths, and purpose?

Only apply if you believe this is a strong potential match and you're willing to put in the focus and effort to win. Then proceed with confidence to demonstrate your experience in light of the role.

Switching sectors.

—

I'm a fan of vertical learning curves. Switching your sector of work—say, from corporate to nonprofit, or engineering to academia, or government to industry—is almost certain to give you a steep learning curve. That drives major professional growth. Go for it!

Be aware, however, that hiring teams tend to make safe choices. They tend to select candidates who have experience that corresponds to what's in the job description. Even if your background maps to a job that's beyond your current experience, level, or sector, keep in mind you'll be competing with people already in the space who may seem like a safer choice for the hiring manager.

To compete, develop your narrative and explicitly connect your background with the main elements of the position. Provide specific examples. Explain why you are the right choice for the role by showcasing your relevant strengths and the value you would bring.

Whenever possible,
choose a vertical learning curve.

As always, a warm introduction is helpful. Once you've begun the interview process, take time to link your skills and accomplishments with the key responsibilities. Search committees rarely "connect the dots," so you have to do that for them. Present your background in light of their organization and role. Offer examples related as closely as possible to the key needs of the position. The less they perceive that your background relates to their needs, the less likely you are to progress in the search.

The most breathtaking vertical leap I made in my career was going from managing a team of eight in a U.S. corporate environment to leading a team of over 100 in a global nonprofit. It never would have happened without a warm introduction, relevant background synergies, and luck. The introduction came from a mentor who served on the organization's board. Synergies included years living overseas in Japan and experience marketing well-known brands. The luck stemmed from the search firm's difficulty finding solid candidates that matched the position description, which made them more open to a background like mine.

Don't go in it unless you're willing to go all in.

Moving outside your comfort zone and taking on a whole new discipline in a new space generates a vertical learning curve, which is hard at first but incredibly rewarding.

Thinking like a hiring committee.

—

Most hiring committees genuinely want to select the best candidate, regardless of where they come from. The pool of candidates may include people already in the organization and individuals recommended by people known to the hiring manager or committee. It's up to you to show them how what you bring is what they need. An introduction certainly helps. A tailored resumé and cover letter are essential. Knowing the stages of a competitive search—and showing up strong at each phase—is also critical.

The winning candidate will demonstrate they understand the bullseye and provide relevant accomplishments. Once the hiring team sees you as a potential match, it can be intangibles like connection to the organization, experiences (e.g., relevant travel, education, internships), and personality traits that help you stand out in a competitive search.

Working with career gaps.

—

Life happens. Most of us will have a break from full-time employment at some point, for whatever reason. When it's time to jump back into a full-time job, you'll find that some employers are skittish about the gap. Knowing that, it's best to provide an explanation that can ease any concerns. Here are ways to overcome the perception that you might not be up to the job due to your time away from full-time employment, relative to candidates who have been in the workforce continually:

- Fill the gap in your resumé (truthfully) with alternative work you did during that period, such as consulting, volunteer work, or developing a business.

- Be ready to explain the gap with a clear, pithy explanation of why you were out and what you did during the time.

- Inoculate yourself upfront by proactively mentioning and explaining the gap. Answer the question before it's asked. That way, you remove it from their list of possible concerns.

Michelle realized that her four-year gap would be worrisome to the hiring team.

It was critical for Michelle to help the hiring team recognize her very relevant experience and how it would apply to their current needs. While not in the immediate past, her years at a high-growth organization similar to BHF were very consequential and analogous to the position she felt ready to take on now. She had also had earlier jobs that demonstrated her competence and other sought-after qualities. Michelle highlighted accomplishments and experiences that resonated in light of the bullseye for the position.

She tailored her resumé to the specifics of the position. When she introduced herself during the interview, Michelle proactively addressed her years away from full-time work—the rationale, and what she accomplished during those years. She stressed her readiness and excitement about jumping back into a growing, fast-paced organization. In a crisp, accessible way, she "connected the dots" between her background and their needs.

Succeeding as an "out of the box" candidate.
—

Hiring committees like to see out of the box candidates, but they rarely hire them. As intriguing as it can be to compete for a role that's outside your areas of strength and expertise, before you put in the time and energy to applying, consider the likely pool of candidates.

Ironically, the way out of the box candidates can prevail is by demonstrating that there is less of a gap between their abilities and those being sought for the position. Josh closed the gap by deepening his knowledge about the desired position and by pointing to relevant synergies in his background:

Josh had always yearned to work in marketing. His background in sales was impressive, but hiring teams kept passing him by for marketing roles as they pictured him as more external and transactional than internal and strategic.

It's harder, but possible, to succeed as an out of the box candidate.

Josh decided to learn more about the marketing discipline. He interviewed a friend who worked in marketing communications and gained some relevant experience by volunteering at a marketing conference. He shadowed someone in the marketing department of his company who taught him how target audiences are chosen, how marketers reach potential customers, and how brand strategies are developed. Josh signed up for a marketing course at a local college.

When a marketing position opened up in his friend's company, Josh asked for an introduction and applied. He prepared for the interview by studying the job description and developing examples of how his successes in sales reflected an understanding of strategic positioning and his understanding of the target audience. He noted his own professional progression toward marketing and his passion for working full-time in the discipline.

If you're not sure whether to apply because you are an out of the box candidate, ask yourself:

- Can I demonstrate competence or synergies relative to most of the skills and experiences they are seeking?
- Why should they choose me over others with more obvious relevant experience?
- What examples or narratives can I provide to help close the gap?

If you believe you have a true path and this could be a great match, proceed! But keep in mind that the more out of the box your background, the harder it will be to prevail over candidates with more of the assets being sought.

Tailoring a strong resumé.

—

In today's competitive market, you stand out by connecting your strengths, values, and background to the needs of the hiring entity. A strong, tailored resumé is the first step. Use your resumé to tell the story of your career trajectory and demonstrate how your strengths make you a compelling prospect.

Here are the top three goals of your resumé:

- Provide a *clear chronology* of your career to date, culminating with current or most recent.
- Showcase relevant background and expertise that qualify you for *this position.*
- Highlight significant accomplishments and experience *relevant to this role.*

You know you're a great match for a position. Now you have to help the recruiter and hiring committee see that. The resumé is the starting point. They will be screening many resumés and considering a variety of backgrounds. It's up to you to help them see you as a contender. That means clearly connecting your experience to their needs by customizing your resumé. If the resumé doesn't highlight the fit, you can kiss the chance at an interview goodbye. Before any conversations occur, your resumé (and, to a lesser degree, your cover letter) do the talking for you.

Initial resumé screenings are completed in less than a minute, so effectively highlighting your relevance to the specific position matters. Your resumé provides the narrative of your career journey to date. It must demonstrate, in a compelling way, the experience and expertise that brings you to this opportunity.

Often the first reader is an Applicant Tracking System (ATS) or other Artificial Intelligence (AI) screener. It pays to embed key words and phrases from the position description, as well as quantifiable accomplishments, in your resumé. Once the resumé passes that screen, a human reader will scan and sort it based on the degree of the perceived match.

Action verbs power up your resumé.

Many candidates get AI help in developing the resumé and refining their narrative and answers. Often AI offers crisp, creative alternative verbiage. However, generalities and inaccuracies often creep in so you need to be the final editor of any AI-generated material.

Your resumé works against you if it is unfocused or hard to

track. Don't lead with a set of competencies unrelated to your work chronology. That will make it hard for the hiring team to understand your career trajectory. If you add details with no apparent relevance to the job, you risk rejection by the ATS or being perceived as a jack-of-all-trades. Hiring committees are turned off by a generalist presentation. Don't send a resumé that leaves them wondering: "Is the candidate interested in this specific position or just looking for a job?"

Your resumé should clearly list your chronological positions, starting with the most recent. Don't lead with "competencies" or list accomplishments unmatched with chronological work. As a headhunter, I skim by the competencies in search of chronology. I want to know where the individual has worked, for how long, and with what results. What was different and better due to their work?

Action verbs fuel your resumé with energy and clarity. Use power words like *led, elevated, enabled, initiated, drove, transformed, increased, grew,* and *achieved.* Choose nouns and adjectives that are evocative, maybe even provocative, and prove your points with relevant metrics.

Dos:

- Use consistent verb tenses, format, and spacing.

- List concise, bulleted points under each position, up to eight bullets for your current/most recent and fewer bullets for prior roles.

- Provide metrics to quantify accomplishments. Examples: "grew revenues from x to y," "saved $x for the organization," "increased employee satisfaction by x percent," and "implemented new technology in a record x months."

- Feature accomplishments relevant to this opportunity.
- De-emphasize less relevant experience that could detract from your overall story.
- Include brand names and familiar organizations. They add credibility.

Don'ts:
- Never use passive voice, such as "was promoted" or "was relocated."
- Don't settle for generalities. Aim for clear and compelling.
- Don't add details and phrases that distract from your narrative for the specific position.
- Never allow typos. Proofread, check spelling, and ask a friend to review your work. Some employers view even a minor typo as evidence of sloppiness, warranting automatic disqualification. Ouch!
- Don't let your design look cluttered or confusing. Make it easy to follow and use basic type, 11 points or larger.
- Don't use more than one second color.
- Don't have a resumé that looks like a sales piece. Glitz gives the impression you're covering up weak qualifications.

Your resumé will not win you the job, but it can work against you. Despite the improvements in screening technology, the basics of resumé writing, and even the physical format, have not changed significantly. Yes, keywords and phrases now factor more heavily in passing you through screening systems to an actual human being. The basics—a clear presentation of relevant experience—still matter most.

Crafting a compelling cover letter.

—

Although not always necessary, a cover letter or "letter of interest" is advisable. Except in rare cases, the letter should be one or two pages in length, not a lengthy dissertation. Use it to communicate interest and the essence of *why you are right for the position*. As with your resumé, tailor what you highlight to the opportunity.

While cover letters draw less attention than resumés, an arresting, well-written letter can boost a candidate's chances. Unlike a resumé, a letter of interest affords you the chance to communicate passion and personal connection to the organization and its work. Here are three instances where winning candidates gained extra traction from a targeted, well-crafted cover letter that made a strong connection with the hiring organization:

- "I am a child of the moss, magnolias, and murky Mississippi . . . " (for an environmental organization).
- "I came in first in your fundraising 5K . . . " (for an organization that puts on events).
- "Graybeard [name of a gorilla] charged through the trees and knocked me off my feet . . . " (for an animal mission).

As with your resumé, think smart about how you customize your letter. AI can help with ideas and crisp summaries, but a generic or unenthusiastic cover letter will fall flat and may harm your chances of advancing. In a worst-case scenario, which I've seen more than once, a candidate re-used a cover letter and failed to replace the name of the organization in the final sentence. That's a non-starter.

Amping up your resumé and cover letter.

—

As we've highlighted throughout the book, to secure a position you love requires focus and intentionality. It starts with discerning who you are now and what you're meant to do, and targeting opportunities that align with your animators, strengths, and purpose. When possible, find your way in through people. Tailor your resumé. Choose arresting language and communicate excitement in your cover letter.

Here's how Michelle approached this:

> Michelle designed her resumé and her cover letter to deliver a focused, compelling message: "I am an experienced finance executive in complex, high-growth contexts like yours." Her cover letter spoke to passion for environmental sustainability and highlighted experience relevant to the bullseye.

Present your experience clearly and chronologically.

She secured an interview. In advance, she prepared examples of the measurable difference she had made in her role at a similar, fast-paced organization. She focused her examples on situations similar to those BHF might expect her to handle. She prepared diligently for each of several increasingly deep interviews, with carefully-chosen examples to underscore how she had handled much of what was needed in the job.

Michelle prepared thoughtful questions for each

meeting. These questions, and the specific examples she shared, were customized for the different groups with whom she interviewed. As the process continued, Michelle continually deepened her understanding of BHF's challenges and its culture. She recorded the insights she gleaned from each encounter. With each new interview, she demonstrated growing knowledge, communicated with enthusiasm, and illustrated her abilities with new stories. Michelle was selected. It was a sweet-spot match, and she remained at the organization for a number of years.

How to organize your resumé.

You'll find many resumé writing services, but beware: these services sometimes focus on beautifying your presentation, forefronting general capabilities, or touting achievements without tying them to the chronological positions. The best approach is to present your experience chronologically, starting with your current or most recent role.

While you'll want to customize for each opportunity, here's a simple, preferred way to organize your resumé. Use two or three pages, except in the case of an academic Curriculum Vita (CV), where you're expected to provide a more extensive list of publications and conference presentations.

The following are guidelines, and you may deviate, keeping in mind that your document should lay out the story you want to tell and present the trajectory of your career and accomplishments:

NAME and contact information

BRIEF SUMMARY
- Overall title describing your background. Examples: Sales Management Professional, Chief Information Officer.
- A brief description of your objective and key selling points (three to four lines) with bulleted key competencies (six to eight at most).

PROFESSIONAL EXPERIENCE
- Your positions, in descending chronological order starting with current or most recent.
- Organization name, dates, locations.
- Title of each role held in the organization.
- Under each position, bullet major accomplishments using power verbs and metrics, such as dollars and percentages. Use the most bullets, up to eight, for your most recent role; fewer bullets for prior roles.

  Note: You can group early-career roles, or work in a different profession, under a banner heading. List all your career experiences, as most employers appreciate the versatility of a hybrid background and earlier work may contribute to aspects of the position.

EDUCATION AND PROFESSIONAL DEVELOPMENT
- Academic degrees and years.
- Additional trainings or qualifications (e.g., certifications like CPA or Six Sigma, leadership programs).

  Note: Education and other assets can be attractively presented in a column to the left of your chronological work experience.

SERVICE, PRESENTATIONS, AND RECOGNITION
- Board, volunteer, and other service
- Select presentations, articles, or books
- Awards and recognition

Incorporate keywords and phrases.

Applicant Tracking Systems (ATS) and AI are regular tools for winnowing out under-qualified applicants. Technology enables hiring organizations to sift through many resumés and more quickly identify potential matches. Incorporate keywords and phrases from the job description. Choose *exact* verbiage rather than synonyms. Here's an example of keywords in a communications job description: team manager, investor relations, crisis management, change management, social media experience.

Thinking like a headhunter.

—

I often read a resumé starting from the bottom to get a sense of an individual's journey and trajectory. I want to understand what drives them and how they've navigated through their educational and career paths. I look for evidence of momentum, relevance to the bullseye, and progress throughout their working years. That includes promotions, evidence of increasing responsibilities, and achievements. Are they impressive, relevant to the position? If too many of their accomplishments were years ago, I wonder whether their more productive days are behind them.

I search for what is different or better as a result of the individual's contributions. I appreciate quantifiable accomplishments, such as "led growth from $x to $y." Is what they are best at relevant to the main mandate of this job? If not, they may not love or be terrific at this role. People excel when their work is centered around what animates them, calls upon their strengths, and aligns with their purpose.

As a headhunter, I try to discern whether you will be happy and successful in the position.

These observations inform my impressions of whether an individual would be happy and successful in a given role. In my world, the best result in a search is a "sweet spot match," one in which the candidate's strengths, animators, and personality align beautifully with the organization's needs, values, and culture.

What headhunters like to see in a resumé

What a headhunter appreciates

- Progression, promotions, career momentum.
- Relevant accomplishments and results, especially recent.
- Longevity and tenacity.
- Ongoing personal growth.
- Energy and enthusiasm.
- Clear, concise communication.

What worries a headhunter

- Job-hopping every couple of years.
- Generalities rather than specific accomplishments.
- Competencies or roles rather than positions and successes.
- Excessive verbiage.
- Sloppiness (typos, run-on sentences).

Realizing it's not all about you.

—

In the first stage of a search, the biggest hurdle is being invited to interview. Far more applicants will be eliminated than interviewed. In your initial interview or set of interviews, present yourself *in light of what they are looking for.* You have many assets, but focus on your specific experience that demonstrates you can address their needs and challenges.

Before you interview, consider:

- In what ways do my strengths and background match the bullseye and criteria?
- Why should they hire *me* versus others who will apply?

Ironically, the process of getting hired is "not about you" at first. It's about their needs and aspirations. Once they are convinced that you are a compelling candidate, they will be open to learning more about you.

Tom was deeply drawn to a certain position. Because the description called for some experience he lacked, he knew he would have an uphill battle persuading the hiring committee to meet and ultimately select him versus others with more relevant experience. Here is Tom's story:

Tom studied the position description. He wanted to discern the central mandate of the job and the abilities needed for success. Because he didn't know the organization, Tom was fortunate to find someone who gave him several helpful insights. The organization was a foundation, created by the endowment of a wealthy donor as a way to invest in the community through philanthropy.

Based on the valuable tips from his advisor and information on the foundation's website, Tom hypothesized that the role required a combination of foundation experience, alignment with the donor's mission, and the ability to work harmoniously with the board and staff.

In his conversations with the headhunter, Tom asked perceptive questions and refined his sense of the bullseye. In his interviews, he shared the relevant parts of his background with examples of accomplishments from his stint at another foundation. Though the mission and environment were different, he could point to similarities of process and culture. He emphasized his passion for this foundation's mission, which matched his own sense of purpose, as well as his connection to its location and aspirations for the future.

---

*Getting hired is "not about you"—
at least not in the beginning.*

The hiring committee would learn more about Tom over the course of their search. But at the beginning of the process, Tom understood the importance of helping them appreciate relevant points of connection. The time for broader discussion about everything you would bring is after you become a real contender, i.e., at the later stages of a search. Be patient, prepare, follow their lead. Give them every reason to want to continue engaging with you.

Curating your story: a cautionary tale.

—

Sharon served with distinction for over a decade at a large, respected organization. In her tenth year, she decided she had contributed all that she could, and the timing coincided with other changes in the organization. She decided to seek her next career adventure and chose to depart before securing a new job.

Sharon had a broad, hybrid background. She had worked in corporate, government, and nonprofit settings and boasted many accomplishments. She'd risen through several positions to a generalist role in which she was managing others, but not focusing on one clear set of responsibilities. Sharon had been a chief operating officer, a fundraiser, and the head of several different disciplines, including finance and programs.

Based on her extensive experience and good references, Sharon was confident of quickly landing a great new opportunity; however, she kept coming in second in searches. Why? As Sharon related the full scope of her experience, hiring committees viewed her as multi-talented and impressive. Yet they didn't see her as "the one" for their needs. She kept losing out to other individuals whose experience was narrower because they were seen as the match for the role at hand. Although Sharon had the relevant experience, hiring committees saw her as a "jack of all trades."

As Sharon kept losing out, she grew discouraged. By presenting her broad, general background, she was failing to make the deep connection essential to succeeding in a search. It was painful to face the fact that her approach had been wrong. She was telling people about herself rather than zeroing in on them and tailoring her narrative to the needs of the hiring organization.

Present your background as it relates to the bullseye of the opportunity.

Sharon changed her strategy. She took the time to more deeply research each opportunity of interest and curated her presentation around the main mandate, presenting her experience relevant to this position and this organization. After a hiring committee saw that Sharon had what was needed for their specific opening, they viewed her additional skills as "value-added."

MILESTONE
TARGET THE JOB'S BULLSEYE

Here are some ways to identify the main position requirement. Consider your current or another role with which you are very familiar. What if you were recruiting someone for that role? What is the main experience or ability the successful candidate needs to have?

Now, apply that logic to the new opportunity. Reread the position description and check out the organization's website. What are they seeking? What challenge does the new hire have to address? What major accomplishment will the new person be expected to achieve? Glean insights from someone who knows the industry or organization if possible.

Try to discern:

- What is the current state of affairs for this organization? What is going well? What opportunities and aspirations might they have?
- What are their challenges? What's keeping management awake at night?
- What is the purpose of the job for which I am applying? What experience and accomplishments are they looking for?
- Do I meet the stated qualifications?
- What "soft skills" do they value?

In addition to the main requirements, the hiring committee will be looking for other assets and abilities. Some of these are non-negotiable, such as location, management experience, or a certain degree. They often consider the size and scope of candidate backgrounds, e.g., revenue or membership growth, number of employee reports, breadth of experience, types of organizations, or target audiences. These additional assets are the invisible boxes a hiring committee would like to check. Consider and prepare to hit the bullseye and to check these likely boxes.

Now, assume you've been selected to interview. Brainstorm the questions you would likely be asked and how you would respond. Be prepared to illustrate your answers with specific examples from your work.

Bringing only your "A" game.

—

A search process is rigorous and time-consuming. It requires responsiveness, focus, and attention to detail. If you take a scattered approach, applying for many positions at once, you will struggle to bring any one of those opportunities to fruition. Scatter-shot job hunting squanders your time and is generally ineffective. Only compete for jobs that truly seem like a strong fit. If an opportunity is marginally appealing to you, or the match is a big stretch, pass it by, even if you are recruited for it.

Before any interaction, do your homework. Be prepared to connect your background to the opportunity, answer questions, and provide examples. Always bring a positive attitude and engaging demeanor. Fully answer the questions you are asked, ensuring you communicate your main talking points.

Successful candidates:

- Learn as much as possible about the organization, mandate, and culture.
- Show high interest and increasing depth of understanding throughout the hiring process.
- Ask questions that reflect their interest and insights.
- Demonstrate responsiveness with written and verbal responses.
- Listen well and answer questions fully.
- Stay positive and carefully nuance concerns and criticisms.
- Share specific, relevant examples of accomplishments that demonstrate their capacity to do the job.

• Follow up to thank interviewers and underscore interest.

Here are three cautionary tales. The candidates' backgrounds were impressive, but each fell short of being selected:

• Jan followed a positive initial conversation with a letter of interest that was boilerplate and not tailored to the role. It failed to advance her case. To make matters worse, she had re-purposed a cover letter from a different application and neglected to proofread carefully. The final sentence referenced a different organization—an unforced error. Based on that, the hiring committee concluded she was looking for "a job," rather than "this specific position." They were also critical of her lack of attention to detail, something she would need to be successful. She did not move forward.

Her unforced error revealed she was looking for "a job," not "this specific position."

• Taylor gave impressive examples of accomplishments that demonstrated the assets the hiring committee was seeking. Without hesitation, the committee advanced Taylor to second-round interviews. In the second interview, Taylor reiterated examples from the first interview. When the hiring committee debriefed the second interview, they felt uncertain. "Are those Taylor's only accomplishments?" While other candidates had continued to broaden their knowledge and return with more examples and questions, Taylor did not evolve after the initial conversation. Lack of preparation and passion were noticeable. Taylor did not move forward.

- David aced his first interview; however, in the second interview, he gave vague answers to several questions. He did not provide relevant examples to demonstrate his abilities or accomplishments. In their debrief, the hiring committee expressed concern that David was not specific and didn't really address their questions. They were unconvinced that he could do the job. He did not move forward.

Dos and don'ts.

Winning requires completing each step of the search process with excellence. If you are sloppy, late, or unresponsive, that can upend your chances. Here are some dos and don'ts for candidates:

Dos:
- At each step in the search, show up with energy and enthusiasm, on time and well-prepared.
- Communicate strategically and carefully. Provide any requested summaries, presentations, or references in a timely manner.
- Keep going deeper to understand the hiring organization's situation and how you can add value.

Dont's:
- Don't miss deadlines or details.
- Don't press for information that will come at later

stages of the search. Understand the process and stay within it.

- Don't repeat examples or stories. Keep refreshing your knowledge and communications.

Gauging your communication.

—

If you've ever worked with someone who talks too much or someone whose responses are abbreviated and incomplete, you can imagine that hiring teams can get frustrated with too much or too little communication.

To gauge the appropriate amount of communication, take your lead from the recruiter or hiring manager. They are managing a number of applicants and following a process. Listen to understand and adhere to that process. They will tell you what they need as well as the timeframe. They don't have time for interactions outside the established process.

Envision the search process. Hiring processes have different variations and timelines, but they have certain stages in common, with breaks in between. At each stage, expect a narrowing process in which fewer contenders move forward. Gaps of days or weeks between stages of the process are normal, and communication from the hiring team can be spotty. Be patient.

Typically, the stages of a search process are:

- Gather, organize, and prioritize candidate resumés or applications.
- Narrow to a group of individuals who receive an initial screening.

- Winnow further to candidates for first rounds of interviews, often with one or more panels.
- Focus on a smaller group of contenders for additional
  interviews.
- An offer and negotiations with the selected candidate.

The aperture of communication, and openness to candidate
needs and interests, grows wider in the later stages of the process. Here are some guidelines on dealing with communication
during the search process:

- Be aware of the search process and current stage. Ask
  when to anticipate hearing back.
- Avoid seeming anxious.
- Don't send more information than is requested. Unsolicited materials or recommendations rarely help and
  can be viewed unfavorably.
- Especially in the early stages, the best way to communicate is via timely responses to requests.
- A thoughtful thank-you note is well received.

Choosing to withdraw or go all in.

—

Dropping out. If you realize the fit is not right or discover the
job is less desirable than you thought, withdraw graciously.
Drop out if you realize the culture, people, or situation are not
in alignment with your values and strengths. Is the role set up
for success? Look for clarity about what the position needs to
accomplish and where it is situated in the organization. Is the

hiring manager part of the interview process? Can you meet members of the team at some point in the process? Ask about red flags that emerge.

If answers are vague, concerning, or unavailable, consider withdrawing from the search. If you decide to withdraw, try to do it during the earlier phases of the process. Waiting until the end, especially if you become a finalist, presents problems for the hiring team and can cause ill feelings.

Going all in. Sometimes a job feels like a calling. You feel certain the position is a match and that you have what it takes to succeed. When you know it's the right fit, be courageous. Share your conviction and your reasoning. Show them the value you will bring. Demonstrate why you are the best choice. Bringing focus and passion, all other things being equal, can make the difference between you and another strong candidate. Authentic passion is often a key differentiator.

Being gracious if you come in second. Even if you don't secure the position, you have met new people who can stay in your life and add to your network. Ask for honest feedback. What could you have done better? What did another candidate bring that you did not? Feedback is a gift. If you learn from it, you will do better next time. Never let your disappointment keep you from a gracious final conversation. Remember to express appreciation for the opportunity to be considered, ask for honest feedback, and stay in touch. The new relationship could lead to a helpful referral or new possibility.

TOP TAKEAWAYS

- Understand the bullseye and tailor your resumé, cover letter, and communication around it.
- In the beginning, it's all about them, not you.
- Connect the dots between your experience and this opportunity.
- Provide specific, relevant examples.
- Prepare well for each stage of the search process and bring your A game for each event.
- Ask for feedback and learn from it.

Stand Out to Stand Apart

What separates the candidate who secures the job offer from individuals who are similarly qualified often comes down to three differentiators:

- Being intentional, engaging, and prepared at each stage of the search.
- Communicating "why me" for this specific opportunity.
- Standing out at each phase of the hiring process.

Rule Number 5 is about strategies for standing out, and helping you be that candidate who comes in first.

Dissecting a search.

—

Searches have a beginning, middle, and end. It pays to understand the arc of the search, the hiring decision-makers, and the stakeholders you're likely to meet along the way.

Searches are stressful for candidates, but also for the hiring team. They worry that they might not find the right candidate or hire the wrong person. They know a hiring mistake is expensive and damaging to the organization as well as the credibility of the hiring team. They're aware that bringing in someone new costs more than twice the position's compensation.

Beyond that, hiring team members may not be fully aligned regarding the qualities needed. Building a shared view can take time during the search process, which can slow down the search processes.

A search can take weeks or months depending on the seniority and significance of the hire. As a general rule, the hiring process looks like this:

- Develop the position description with input from key stakeholders such as peers and direct reports.

- Post the description and seek candidates via advertising, proactive recruiting, referrals, LinkedIn, and outreach to relevant networks.

- Use resumé screening and initial calls to create an initial set of possible candidates.

- Narrow the list to those who will be interviewed (usually five to eight candidates).

- Conduct in-person or virtual interviews, generally an

hour each with the hiring team and often other panels.

- Narrow to two to three finalists for deeper interviewing. Finalists are often asked for a written or oral presentation.
- Conduct referencing and background checks.
- Make an offer and negotiate with the selected candidate.

To secure the offer, you need to excel in each stage of the search. Hiring committees look for:

- Relevant experience in similar or analogous contexts.
- Essential skills and strengths, such as professional expertise and ability to accomplish the mandate of the position.
- Human assets, including likability, relational and communication skills, plus fit with the organization's values and culture.

Present your background authentically and convincingly connect your background, accomplishments, and personality to the bullseye. Address the additional needed skill areas as you can. Listen carefully and fully respond to questions. Meet the requests of the search committee with timely, high-quality responses. Help the hiring team and others you meet come to know you, like you, and envision you in the position. Find ways to offer unexpected synergies or added value so you stand out.

Prioritizing assets for the current job market.

—

Every position has core requirements. You won't be hired in technology without coding or other relevant skills, or in marketing without experience in the discipline, including social media. To become in-house general counsel, you'd best be a lawyer. For more senior roles, hiring committees look for relevant accomplishments and consider the size and scope of your experiences in areas such as:

- Leadership skills and strategic acumen.
- Ability to inspire, manage, and motivate teams.
- Record of building or growing revenues, a division, or an organization.
- Change management expertise.

More than ever, people skills are prized, including:

- Emotional intelligence (EQ as well as IQ).
- A collaborative, inclusive way of working.
- Confidence, coupled with humility and a sense of humor.
- Relationship and culture-building skills, including listening and empathy.
- Ability to work cross-functionally and in teams.
- Communication and persuasion skills.
- Charisma, vitality, and likeability.
- Fit with the organization's work, culture, and aspirations.
- Lived experience relevant to the organization's target audiences.

The combination of assets for a given position *plus something above and beyond* is often the winning combination. Examples of "above and beyond" include:

- A unique connection to the organization or deep knowledge of its work or industry.

- A meaningful connection to the geography, history, or mission of the organization.

- A recommendation from someone the organization trusts.

- Relevant additional talents, accomplishments, or experiences, beyond the key needs of the position, that are seen as adding value to the organization.

- Specific experience solving the kinds of issues the organization faces.

- Thoughtful insights or breakthrough ideas, delivered with the humility of an outsider who knows less than people within the organization.

Knowing why you fit.

—

When you see an appealing opportunity, study what they are looking for and analyze the mandate. Examine how your experiences and strengths might relate to the demands of the role, as well as any deficits or learning curves. As you consider whether the position is really a match, and whether you would be competitive with other candidates who would likely be interested, think through:

- Why am I attracted to this position?

- How does it line up with my animators, strengths, and purpose?

- What is the apparent bullseye, and how does my

experience prepare me to hit that? What about the other aspects of the mandate?

- What are the other "boxes" the committee will be seeking to check?
- How does my unique set of assets match the challenges and aspirations of the role?
- What examples from my journey will demonstrate my relevant experience?
- What are other likely candidates going to bring in terms of backgrounds and experiences? How can I be most competitive in that mix?
- How could I stand out?

Be clear about what makes you a strong contender. Know the answer to the question, "Why should they hire me?" As you learn more about the organization, your "why me?" answer may evolve. Be clear-eyed about why and how you're the ideal match. You'd be surprised at how few candidates operate with that clarity.

Telling your unique story.

—

In almost every interview, you'll be invited to introduce yourself. Develop a concise introduction that connects your background to their position. This is also called an "elevator speech" because it's pithy and could be delivered in the duration of an elevator ride. Your elevator speech should highlight your experience, relevant value proposition, and reason for interest in the role.

For a job interview, you will likely provide an elevator speech of one to two minutes. Use your introduction to deliver a compelling narrative that presents:

- Your background and relevant career highlights.
- The reason you're interested in the position.
- Why you believe you're a match for the role.

Your elevator speech is a concise introduction of yourself and your interest in the position.

Your elevator speech should combine self-understanding (relevant strengths, background, purpose) with a persuasive explanation of why you're here and how you see yourself as a strong contender.

To prepare your introduction, decide on a main point and three secondary points you want to make. Prepare and rehearse, but don't memorize. Deliver it as naturally and comfortably as you can. Be prepared to add depth, examples, and details, but keep the initial elevator speech condensed and focused on this opportunity.

MILESTONE
TELL YOUR COMPELLING STORY

Don't wait until the last minute before an interview to prepare your elevator speech introduction. Develop a very short summary of what you do currently, key relevant experience, the reason for your interest, and what makes you right for this specific opportunity. You will customize your introduction for each opportunity.

Making magic.

—

When you reach out to build your network of relationships and ask people for advice, over time the just-right opportunity often appears. Tom had such an experience.

Tom had begun to think about the next step in his career and was seeking advice from colleagues, friends, and others who could help him move toward the fulfilling nonprofit or foundation position he wanted. His broad background included corporate and nonprofit experience as well as work at a grant-making foundation.

This job description was written for me.

One of Tom's advisors suggested a position at a philanthropic, grant-making foundation. Tom read the description and smiled. "This was written for me."

The role was as director of a grant-making foundation. The visionary donor and founder had died unexpectedly and left additional funds for the foundation in his will. The small foundation was about to see a large influx of new funds. The board decided to hire a professional director to ensure the quality of the foundation's work and to lead planning for a sustainable future.

The position description described the opportunity as developing and implementing the foundation's philanthropic giving strategy in a way that reflected "the founding donor's intent and values, the foundation's own heritage, and the community's needs." It noted that the new director would step into a "fluid environment" and would be charged with developing programs and processes to capitalize on the anticipated funds.

Tom found every aspect of the description exciting and consistent with his areas of strength and experience, as well as his desired areas of professional growth. The position called for the director to:

- Lead the foundation in addressing opportunities presented by the impending influx of funds.
- Be an external relationship builder across the community.
- Manage the organization internally.
- Organize and lead grantmaking activity.
- Partner successfully with the board, the staff, grantees, and the broader community.

While Tom lacked experience in some of these areas, especially the first, he had significant relevant experience and expertise. After re-reading the description several times, he felt he understood the main mandate—helping the organization make the most of new funding—and saw himself as the match. This was a leadership role in an organization where his expertise and passion could make a difference and where he felt he would thrive.

As he began interviewing, he realized how comfortable he felt with board members and how excited he was about the mandate. This work was exactly what he was meant to do. Now he had to convince the headhunter and the board that he was the best choice!

He began his self-introduction with these words: "All my life I've been preparing for this job."

To be selected, Tom had to stand out over the course of a long search among a competitive pool of candidates. He had to demonstrate his ability to help the foundation achieve its aspirations for impact in the future. Tom had to employ the patience of a marathon runner who has studied the course and is committed to navigating, persevering, and completing it. He convinced the hiring committee that he was the right match, and he has proven it, again and again, over many years.

Debunking recruiting myths.

—

Recruiting is both an art and a science. Often the selected candidate is someone who has most, not all, of the qualifications being sought. They may demonstrate strong cultural fit and connection to the organization's mission, people, or location.

Here are three myths that deserve to be debunked:

Myth: You must have every qualification listed in the position description.

The truth: A candidate with 75 percent of what's in the job description can win if they're a strong match for the bullseye and the culture. Also, a hiring team's vision of what the position requires can evolve over the course of the search. Don't be afraid to apply if you have most of what's in the mandate.

Myth: If you believe you can do the work, you can win the job without much relevant experience.

The truth: You probably could do it; however, you'll be competing in a pool of candidates that includes people who can demonstrate they've already done most of what's required. Make sure you're competitive in a hypothetical pool of prospects before you take the time to apply.

Myth: The most capable person will be selected.

The truth: Hiring committees pay attention to intangibles (emotional intelligence, communication style, and collaboration skills), compatibility with the culture, as well as experience and skills. Those weigh heavily in the decision because "culture eats strategy for lunch," and no one can succeed if they cannot engage well with an organization's culture.

Translating your why into their what.

—

An appealing position attracts dozens of applicants. Some apply cold online, and in many cases hear nothing in response. Others come into the search as prospective candidates discovered through LinkedIn and other research. Their background may bring them into the search thanks to a recruiter. Still others come to the search through referrals.

The candidate pool for most searches is quite broad and diverse. The individual who is ultimately hired will have strengths and experience relative to the main mandate and other key "boxes" the hiring committee wants to check. The selected candidate will help the hiring committee accurately perceive their relevant strengths and experiences. They will demonstrate alignment with the organization's culture and exhibit the soft skills and most of the hard skills needed. They will connect effectively with the recruiter and the hiring team.

Here is an example of a candidate who translated her interest in the opportunity—her "why"—into the "what" the hiring team was looking for. The job was as an operations leader in a faith-based organization. Theresa's story illustrates the power of focusing on the organization's needs and uniting her why with the position's what:

> Theresa was one of over 150 individuals my search firm contacted for the position. She provided a resumé that showed compatibility between the requirements and her background. In our initial call, she listened well and communicated clearly how her background covered most of what the role required. She asked numerous questions and expressed passion for this kind of work. She explained how her career experiences would help her succeed in this job.
>
> Theresa shared that she had devoted her career to operations, systems, and processes, and it was what she loved. She had technology and facilities management experience (mentioned specifically in the position description) and an undergraduate degree in finance. She described teams she had led. She said she

was animated by engaging with problems, juggling challenges, and devising solutions. She emphasized her desire to apply these strengths in the context of her religious faith.

Theresa provided her career narrative and highlighted her faith journey. Her personal faith resonated with the hiring committee and inspired them to see her as a good fit for the culture. Through several interviews, Theresa presented examples of accomplishments with specific examples relevant to the organization and its challenges. She projected an energizing personality and listened well, answering each question thoroughly. The hiring committee came to see her as the perfect fit.

Who was in the position previously?

If someone has left, been fired, or retired from a position you're interested in, understanding the circumstances provides helpful context. Was the person beloved? What was special about the prior leader's personality and approach? What was missing that the organization would likely want to enhance with this hire?

You can't always gain access to such information, but knowing about the predecessor can provide clues about the team's expectations, hopes, and concerns. The weaknesses of the departed individual are often among the assets being sought in the new hire.

Navigating as an internal candidate.

—

Being an internal candidate affords both advantages and disadvantages. A big advantage is knowing the organization's goals and culture. A disadvantage is that colleagues think of you in your current role and have observed your weaknesses as well as your strengths.

Don't apply until you read the position description. Decide whether or not to apply based on the main assets that description prioritizes. Don't apply unless you are objectively a good fit. Often, a highly talented internal candidate with demonstrated strengths finds they are not a strong match for a role that calls for different skills or experience. For example, a superb operations person is an unlikely choice for a primarily external chief executive role. Throw your hat in the ring if, based on what the hiring team is prioritizing, you can be a strong contender within a pool of candidates that includes people who currently hold similar positions in other organizations.

Applying as an internal candidate can be stressful. If you decide to apply, here are tips based on many searches with inside candidates. Some were selected, others were not.

- Don't talk much, or even at all, to your colleagues about the fact you're applying. It can harm your prospects of being selected if you become a focus of speculation or gossip.

- Be prepared for the possibility that, in a competitive pool of candidates, you are not chosen. How will you deal with it? Can you remain at the organization? Can you overcome any negative feelings and work with the outside hire?

- Prepare for your interview by envisioning yourself in the new job. Dress the part, act the part, and speak on topics relevant to the new position rather than your current role. Don't let the hiring team "talk shop" with you. Remain focused on your candidacy.

Impressing the interview team.

———

Interviews take place at various stages of a search. Each has a somewhat different purpose and often involves a different interviewer or panel. Each stage presents an opportunity that warrants thorough preparation. Know the purpose, context, and sequencing of these opportunities so you can prepare accordingly. Do your homework about the interviewer(s), the organization, and the opportunity. Prepare and tailor your elevator speech. Prepare questions relevant to this interviewer or group. Prepare to flex, be relatable, be likable, be yourself, and wow at each interview stage.

Most interviews fall into one of these categories:

- **A courtesy interview** is not connected to a specific search but usually results from a warm introduction by someone in your network. It could be an audition for a potential search. It's an opportunity to request advice, to cultivate a relationship, or to garner additional warm introductions. If you wow in a courtesy interview, your search may advance in unexpected ways.

   How to wow: Come off as memorable, radiate talent, and identify a follow-up, such as a promised referral. Make a promise and keep it.

- **A screening interview** is the first conversation with a recruiter or hiring team. Prepare by researching the organization and the position. They are trying to determine whether you qualify for further conversations. If you wow them, you move to the next interview.

  How to wow: Prepare! Demonstrate how your background aligns with the job description. Listen carefully to address questions and give detailed examples as requested.

Know how to wow.

- **Interviews for a search** often start with a panel. This *team interview* is conducted by the hiring/search committee or a group of relevant stakeholders. It focuses on acquainting the group with your experience *relative to the position.* After your self-introduction (your elevator speech), you can expect questions like: "Tell me about a time when you..." or "Describe how you ...". This is a *behavioral interview.*

  How to wow: Give a compelling self-introduction relevant to the position and your sense of the match. Then, pay close attention to their needs and questions. Answer with concise examples. Demonstrate that you understand what's needed and have dealt with the scope and challenges similar to what they've described.

- **In-depth interviews** take place at later stages of a search, with group and one on one meetings. These are designed to check for chemistry and to further test whether you are a suitable match. They want to learn more about your strengths, personality, animators, thought processes, and culture fit. You may be given a writing assignment, a presentation, or a problem-solving case study. They may invite deeper discussions and questions, possibly over a meal. You may meet with several individuals or groups, including the hiring manager and people you would work with.

How to wow: Connect on an interpersonal level. They are looking for the right partner. Be yourself, be human, be likable. Make your presentations insightful and authentic. Research and mention synergies around the work, colleges, hometowns, etc. Ask probing questions. Demonstrate self-confidence as well as humility.

- **References** are requested only from the handful of final candidates, so it's a great sign if you're asked for them. Glowing endorsements provide third-party validation. They can be powerful and determinative. Headhunters and hiring teams can be swayed by references' enthusiasm, relevant examples, and recommendations. Typically, hiring teams ask for "360-degree" references: people you've reported to, supervised, or worked with as a peer.

How to wow: Curate your references based on the organization. Select individuals they respect, including people they know if possible. Let the references know they will be called and share your enthusiasm for the opportunity as well as specific qualities the hiring team is seeking.

In addition to preparing for, performing well, and following up at each stage of a search, look out for special wow opportunities. If over the course of the search you receive an award or media coverage, publish an article, or interview on a podcast, absolutely share that. But don't over-communicate. Take your cues from the recruiter or hiring committee, and always follow up and stay positive.

Why headhunters ask, "Describe a time when you..."

Many recruiters, including me, have faith in the proposition that "the best indicator of what someone will do is often what they have done." It's not always the case, but often a candidate's history—including longevity in a certain type of position or organization—is at least partially predictive of their animators, strengths, and what they will bring to a new position.

In the early interview stages, we tend to avoid hypothetical questions like, "How would you tackle such-and-such issue..." in favor of questions that ask for past accomplishments and work style, such as "Tell me about a time when you had to deal with an issue like such-and-such...".

Once we believe you have the experience and background needed for the position, we are ready for vision questions and "What would you do..." scenarios. But most of us begin our initial set of questions with phases like "Tell me about a time when..." or "Describe how you..." so we can learn what you have already done that's relevant to the position.

"How would you" hypotheticals and questions

about your vision for the job come later. In combination, robust behavioral and hypothetical questions help hiring committees understand you more comprehensively.

Preparing for the Top 10 interview questions.

—

Interviewers ask all kinds of questions, but most begin by inviting you to introduce yourself. That's your cue to provide your elevator speech, one or two minutes, tailored to the opportunity. Be sure to both prepare well and sound unrehearsed.

Later, you'll likely be asked behavior-based questions ("tell me about a time when...") related to the position itself. To prepare, closely read the job description again. Envision the bullseye and additional strengths or experience they may value. Prepare specific examples. For instance, if the position calls for "a team builder," prepare one or more relevant examples with quantifiable examples when possible, such as "we raised employee satisfaction scores from x to y" or "my ratings from staff are in the top 10 percent."

Here are frequently-asked interview questions:

- What attracts you to this opportunity? How do you see yourself as a match for this?
- What accomplishments are you most proud of?
- How do you make decisions? How do you build consensus? How do you bring people together?
- How have you built collaboration, consensus, unity, cohesion? How have you dealt with conflict?

*The best indicator of what someone
will do is what they have done.*

- Describe a failure and how you dealt with it. What did you learn?

- What do team members like about working with you? What do they wish you'd do differently? How would they describe your leadership (or management) style?

- Describe a complex problem, conflict, or difficult situation you have dealt with. How did you handle it? What was the result?

- How have you led change or transformation? What were the results? How have you overcome resistance?

- What is your ideal work environment? What kind of culture do you thrive in? What kind of culture do you create?

- What aspects of your current position animate you? Which are the most difficult? What does a great day look like for you?

Inoculating yourself against concerns.

—

There is no perfect candidate, of course. The hiring team will have concerns and questions about each potential hire. The secret is to anticipate their major concerns about you and "inoculate" yourself in advance. You do that by preemptively raising the issue and providing a simple explanation before the hiring committee asks about it. Addressing a potential concern puts you in control and prevents you from operating on the defensive. Prepare a concise sentence or two about any issue(s) that might worry the hiring team. Often it helps to include your explanation as part of your introduction to take the issue off the table.

Here are some examples of frequent hiring team concerns, and preemptive statements that work to inoculate you:

Concern: Short tenures (two years or less) in recent positions.

Statement: In recent years, I've had several opportunities arise. I've made faster moves than I would have preferred. I'm eager to make a commitment for the long haul now.

Concern: Geographic and career moves.

Statement: My spouse works in a corporate role that has required several moves in the past. We are settled here now, and we don't anticipate another relocation.

Concern: Gap in employment.

Statement: I took a break from full-time work to address family health/other issues. The situation is resolved. I'm energized and ready to jump back in at full speed.

Following the Top 10 interview tips.

—

A great interview connects, engages, and persuades. It demonstrates why the candidate is a strong potential hire. If you follow these tips, you'll always perform well.

- Be warm, likable and authentic—a person people would want to work with.

- Maintain comfortable eye contact. Treat everyone equally, respectfully, and seriously.

- Prepare and deliver a compelling elevator speech. "Why me?"—why you're interested and a good fit for this opportunity. Avoid seeming rehearsed. Make it memorable and differentiating.

- Listen closely and follow the hiring team's lead. They have questions they need to ask. Answer concisely and fully, with a relevant example.

- Present your experience in light of their needs. Show how your background and strengths match their situation.

- Use examples to demonstrate relevant experience. When a hiring committee declines to move a candidate forward, they often cite "lack of specific examples." They didn't see evidence that the candidate could do what they needed.

- Prepare the top three points you must make to persuade the team that you are the match for the position. Include these points in your introduction and weave them into your interview responses.

- Surprise them with the depth of your research and insights. Be modest about what you don't know, too.

- Show interest and passion for this opportunity. Genuine enthusiasm is a powerful persuader. Hiring committees are looking for someone who will commit to their organization rather than a "job seeker."

- Tailor your questions to the group you're meeting with.

Keep in mind the committee is seeking a colleague and a partner who will do great work and align well with their values and culture. Here are some interview dos and don'ts:

Dos:
- Dress as well or more formally than the hiring team.
- Answer their specific questions fully, citing examples.
- Demonstrate how your background aligns with the organization's needs.
- Prepare questions appropriate to the interview team. Some questions are appropriate for the board, others for peers, others for staff.
- Keep learning throughout the interview process.
- Arrive on time, follow up in a timely way, make responses clear and typo-free.

Don'ts:
- Don't act like you already have the solutions or a vision. Offer ideas, but be humble.
- Don't elaborate with excessive details or share long stories.
- Don't overlook or override their questions.
- Don't tell the same story twice.
- Don't let down your guard.

Curating your references.

—

Hold off on providing references until they are requested. You should curate your list to make it relevant to the position you are seeking. When an organization asks for your references, that's a sign you are a real contender. Often, they will want contact information for five or six people who have worked with you or know you well. That typically includes people you've reported to, supervised, or worked with as a peer. What your references say, how they say it, and how enthusiastically they respond to the reference request can be differentiating for you.

Provide the most recent, relevant references for this specific position. When possible, include current colleagues who can maintain confidentiality. Curate your list based on this position's needs, industry, location, issues, and people that will make your references stand out to the hiring committee. Based on this specific opportunity, who can provide a detailed reference that addresses the position mandate and the concerns of the hiring team? If you know someone the hiring committee already respects, that's a perfect name for your list. Smart hiring teams will likely contact a recent former employer and one or two informal references who can maintain confidence, whether you provide their names or not.

Make sure your references know to expect a call from the hiring team. Let them know the position mandate and why you believe this is the right fit. Invite them to offer their honest assessment and thank them in advance.

Generating that "something extra."

—

The candidate who lands the offer connects especially well to the hiring team and needs of the organization. "Something extra" differentiates you, whether that's your experiential depth in the bullseye needs, a special talent, a notable accomplishment, or a deep connection to the substance of the position.

In ways that don't overstep the process or over-communicate, try to offer something more, something beyond what the hiring team expects. Here are some examples:

- Look for "invisible boxes" you might check—assets the hiring team may not be consciously seeking but which are additive. They may be ancillary to the main needs but potential differentiators, for example: unique lived experiences; narrative about your purpose or sense of call; linguistic, cultural, or technology competencies that could add value.

"Invisible boxes" can include relevant lived experiences

- Without being presumptuous that you already have solutions, share hypotheses that demonstrate you're thinking about issues they're wrestling with. Show how you might approach those. Help them envision a positive organizational outcome if you apply your energy and talents.

- Demonstrate a deeper level of connection and shared experiences. Read interview team bios and seek out connections. Read between the lines and sense in your gut what they really need.

- Surprise them with something in your background that is intriguing, humorous, or unusual. Be memorable and enjoyable.

- Demonstrate at each interview that you care about them and their issues. For example, one candidate won over the staff by asking exceptionally thoughtful questions tailored to the staff's perspectives.
- Be the candidate who best demonstrates you can "meet us where we are and take us where we want to go."

Winning over everyone.

—

Headhunters are engaged to identify candidates who meet an organization's needs. They work with the hiring team to define the position, recruit broadly to find strong prospects, and help the organization recruit the best match for its needs.

Headhunters understand the mandate for the position, as well as the culture, challenges, and aspirations of the organization. Ask them questions. They are experts in helping you evaluate the opportunity and position yourself. Rather than advocate for individual candidates, headhunters are charged with presenting several good options and helping the hiring team evaluate them. While they shy away from recommending a specific candidate, their enthusiastic presentation of your strengths can influence the hiring committee's thinking.

Headhunters are accustomed to conversing with many types of people on an ongoing basis, so they're easy to talk with. Be straightforward in answering their questions. Be professional, clear-spoken, and likable. Help them see how your experience, strengths, and personality are a match for the position. Don't underestimate the influence of the headhunter. They make the decision on which candidates to present to the client. Don't be rude, dismissive, or unlikable.

A cautionary tale

Jonathan was interested in a search I was conducting. He had experience relevant to the opportunity, so I scheduled time to interview him. I asked questions to understand how his background met the position criteria and to gauge how his personality might fit with the organization's inclusive culture. Jonathan was dismissive of my questions and seemed impatient to move on past me and meet with the hiring committee. He saw me as an impediment rather than a resource who could help him succeed in the search. Some of his answers were condescending.

When someone shows you who they are, believe them.

Jonathan's disrespect revealed a personality trait that was disqualifying for a job that required positive collaboration across the organization at all levels. While he had relevant abilities, he didn't match the position based on fit with the organization's values and culture. I could not recommend him to the hiring committee.

As Maya Angelou wrote, "When someone shows you who they are, believe them the first time."

When I called Jonathan back to let him know he wasn't moving forward in the search, he berated me: "I can't believe you're not giving me a chance to win over the client." My response: "If you couldn't win over the headhunter, what makes you think you could have won over the client?"

The headhunter represents the client's interests. They will ask tough questions to determine whether you could be a match. If the recruiter doesn't believe you have the right assets, that's it: you will not advance to meet the client. Show the headhunter your best side. Convince them you are a worthwhile prospect.

Behind the scenes: A day in the life of a headhunter.

—

Headhunters are busy and booked, juggling multiple searches at a time. Whatever search you're interested in is one of many searches they're managing. If you are a potential candidate with a solid background, the headhunter will consider you, but making it onto their calendar can be a challenge. When you talk with them, be prepared. Your goal is to convince them you're a viable contender and to learn as much as you can about the organization and role.

What does a day in the life of a headhunter look like? Here is my schedule for a recent day:

Kathy's schedule on a typical Thursday.

Time	Activity
7-8 a.m.	Organize the schedule and day's priorities. What needs to move today? I organize by client, new business, meetings, and interviews.
8-8:30 a.m.	Interview a potential candidate.
8:30-9:30 a.m.	Initiate outreach to potential candidates and referral sources. Schedule calls and respond to questions. Finalize and send a search update to a client.
9:30-10 a.m.	Talk with a client about search strategy.
10-11 a.m.	Conduct 30-minute interviews with two prospective candidates. Add notes to the relational database.
11-11:45 a.m.	Meet a potential new client that is evaluating search firms (a "new business pitch").
12-1:30 p.m.	Eat lunch while preparing a report. Return calls from referral sources, potential candidates, and a current client. Call a colleague to discuss a search challenge.
1:30-5:00 p.m.	Host candidate interviews via Zoom. The first 30 minutes is preparing the search committee (seven people in this case), which includes deciding who will ask each question. Each of three interviews lasts an hour, followed by the search committee debrief on likes and concerns.

5:00-5:30 p.m.	Reach out to the candidates to let them know where they stand in the search.
5:30-6 p.m.	Call a candidate in a different search to prepare them for their interview next week.
6-6:30 p.m.	Complete undone tasks for the day. Prepare for the next day.

My work as a headhunter aligns with my animators, strengths, and purpose. I feel energized and engaged throughout each day. I enjoy:

- Leaning into conversations with candidates, current clients, and potential new clients. Each individual, situation, and topic is unique and stimulating in some way.
- Having opportunities to coach, make recommendations, and ask questions.
- Identifying high-quality potential candidates for clients.
- Working with candidates to help them understand the opportunity and prepare for interviews and next steps.
- Moving searches forward toward successful conclusions.

Receiving a job offer.

—

Congratulations on getting the offer! Searches can take months to conclude, and the process often involves multiple steps, twists, and turns. At each stage, you've had to demonstrate why you're the match for this position at this time. Simultaneously, you have learned about the opportunity, people, and organizational culture. Your hard work has paid off!

Before you say yes, consider that this is the moment when the balance of power shifts in your favor. They have decided they want to hire you. Now it's your turn to advance any questions you have and ensure your needs can be met. Now is the time to confirm that this is, indeed, the match and to negotiate for any changes that will ensure your success. Consider:

- Do you have questions about the culture, responsibilities, or expectations? Ask for more information or additional people to meet.

- Have you met a cross-section of your future colleagues, including the person you'll report to, future peers, and direct reports? Establishing good rapport is essential to your success. Ask to meet them.

- Are the compensation and benefits reasonable, given the responsibilities? In addition to the base salary, understand the health, vacation, paid leave, in-office, and other elements. Negotiate as needed.

Offers are usually made verbally at first to confirm your interest and likelihood to accept, and then in writing. If it feels right, go ahead and give a conditional yes while sharing any initial concerns and reserving time to review the offer in writing before accepting. You basically have four options:

- Accept and finalize terms and dates.

- Negotiate for more favorable terms. Let them know what it will take for you to accept.

- Request more time to consider the offer, possibly asking for additional information or conversations.
- Decline respectfully and express your gratitude for the opportunity.

Now is your chance to negotiate.

"No one wants change but a wet baby."

—

Before you say yes to a new position, try to discern the amount of change needed and the organization's readiness for change. How strong are the commitment and backbone of organizational leadership? How aligned are you with their vision? Will leadership have your back, even amidst the inevitable complaints that accompany change?

Creating change can be very challenging. As one candidate said: "No one wants change but a wet baby." Even when people agree on the "burning platform" that necessitates change, internal resistance as change is enacted can be fierce. An incoming leader is wise to begin with a period of listening, consensus-building, and preparation before initiating major changes.

Deciding when to say no.

—

The worst outcome of a search, for you and the hiring organization, is a mismatch. The result is a short or unhappy tenure, which will disrupt your career trajectory and the organization. Don't wait until you have an offer to evaluate how fully the opportunity matches your animators, strengths, and purpose. Continually assess the job requirements and the work culture over the course of the search. If you conclude it's actually a non-ideal match, don't hesitate to withdraw graciously. Unless last-minute discoveries cause your decision to decline an offer, make your "no" decision before you receive an official offer.

If it's not right, withdraw
before you receive an offer.

Succeeding in most positions requires collegial relationships and a true fit with the culture. Even if your mandate is to change the culture, you won't progress unless you start by "meeting people where they are." Insist on scheduling time with those you will work closely with. If your gut indicates a mismatch, pay attention. Here are some ways to assess the potential match:

- Insist on meeting those you will work with. Ask questions and sense the culture.

- Consider what the new hire is expected to achieve. Are the opportunities, and the challenges, in sync with your animators and strengths?

- Interrogate the risks and downsides of the position. What has been the rate of turnover recently? How are the finances? What's being reported by departed staff on Glassdoor?

- Learn about the organization's leadership, business model, and likely future. What are the prospects for the future?
- Look objectively at the opportunity: Do you see potential to learn, grow, and thrive in the organization?

Own your power to shape how you're perceived.

Owning your power.

—

Standing out in a competitive market isn't just about experience and skills. It's about presenting your unique value in a way that resonates with the hiring team and others you meet. Develop and practice your personal narrative and examples of accomplishments relevant to the opportunity. Own your power to shape how you're perceived. Figure out and communicate what sets you apart.

Winning an offer is the result of communicating effectively and consistently, demonstrating good fit and chemistry, and helping the hiring team see your potential as well as your competence and experience. Focus your message, stand out, and wow the hiring team. You will land a job you love.

TOP TAKEAWAYS

- Decide why you are the match for this opportunity and why the hiring team should choose you over other candidates.
- Prepare specifically to wow at each interview and at each stage of the search.

- Find a way to personally connect with each interviewer and panel you meet.

- Ask insightful questions relevant to each interviewer.

- Prepare answers and examples for job-specific questions as well as the Top 10 interview questions.

Love the Journey

Finding work you love rather than just a job requires intentionality. As one of my colleagues puts it, "Take charge of your career—or someone else will." Work consumes up to a third of your time. Something you spend that much time on deeply affects your overall happiness and sense of well-being. Taking charge matters!

Headhunter Confidential is about helping you take charge and thrive. I hope you will find adventure in the journey, satisfaction and growth in your work, and terrific people along the way. The happiest people on earth find joy in each part of their lives: relationships, recreation, hobbies, learning, and work.

At different stages of life, your "perfect job" will vary. When you're just starting out, you are wise to join a bustling enterprise with role models and mentors and a variety of growth experiences.

As you progress, leadership and management challenges may engage your imagination and refine your skills. In later years, you may find exciting new opportunities to contribute, certainly as a mentor, and possibly in consulting or leadership positions that leverage your experience.

Take charge of your career—or someone else will.

The rules in this book help you define your "perfect" position and take charge of your career at each stage. With each time of change, reconsider "who am I, and what do I want in my work now?" As you fashion a career, you are building relationships and a track record, so keep the long term in mind. The people you have worked with and will work with in the future are important relationships. They are sources of growth and connection.

When you find your new position, remember to thank everyone who helped you get there. Then plan your entry strategy. Starting strong helps ensure your success over time. Later, you will plan your exit strategy and the glidepath to your next adventure.

Navigating a satisfying journey.

—

Across the arc of your career, you may work in a variety of organizations across different sectors. Hopefully, you will find increasingly good matches for your animators, strengths, and purpose. I hope that with each new opportunity, you discover more of what you love and leave behind elements you don't enjoy. You now know the unwritten rules for landing a job you love and strategies to win at each stage:

- Adopt the right mindset.
- Set a clear direction.
- Connect with people.
- Focus on the bullseye.
- Stand out to stand apart.
- Love the journey.

With each new opportunity, I hope you will lean in and take risks. Even if you remain in the same organization for years, set an intention to grow and experiment. Set the goal that, with each change, a higher percentage of your working hours will animate you and draw on your strengths.

Learning from successful job-changing stories.

—

Early in the book, we introduced seven individuals who sought a new job opportunity and their different starting points: job loss or threat, a toxic environment, values or culture mismatch, boredom or need to grow, new life circumstances, re-starting after a break, or just starting out. Throughout the book, we learned about the journeys of these job-seekers and others looking for fulfilling work. Let's check back in on the seven transitions:

Bouncing back from termination: Drew's journey.

After fifteen years with a large, public company, Drew was fired by a new supervisor who did not value his marketing skills or reputation as a "fixer" who could solve problems across the organization.

After taking time for a mental reset, Drew decided to rekindle his passion for the arts. Early in his career, right after college, he was a standup comedian. He had worked with various theaters and toyed with a career in the arts but instead navigated in the more lucrative direction of engineering.

Drew knew it would be close to impossible to bridge his career from a large corporate entity to a nonprofit arts organization with no recent relevant experience. He began contacting everyone he knew in the arts community, including marketing and fundraising professionals. They told him to start by volunteering, so he took on volunteer ushering roles and started attending more events and concerts, visiting museums, and meeting people in those contexts.

He was fortunate to meet a fundraising staff person at his city's symphony. The organization had an open marketing position, and she encouraged Drew to apply. His sense of humor and passion for classical music helped them see Drew as a potential hire.

Facing impending overseas travel and the crush of a new symphony season, the hiring manager advanced Drew in the search. Sure, he had much to learn, but he was smart and had a valuable track record in other contexts. Drew was highly motivated, and everyone he met liked him. The symphony hiring team decided to give him a chance.

This was the start Drew needed in a completely different sector, and he mastered the learning curve with energy and creativity. In a couple of years, another arts organization recruited him. Several years later, he evolved further to take a fundraising and team leadership role at another nonprofit. Building on his fundraising and other management experience, Drew continued to grow professionally. He is now CEO of an organization that advises nonprofits. All of these opportunities originated with a pink slip.

Fleeing a toxic culture: Angela's resolve.

Angela's organization had developed a toxic culture. Though the work was in healthcare, the organization had not intervened to stop a group of influential staff members from becoming a powerful clique and creating an environment of exclusion, low support, and high anxiety. Micro-aggressions became a daily issue, and Angela's physical and mental health were suffering. She debated the pros and cons of speaking out and asking for help. As a single mom, Angela could not afford to be out of work. Nor was she comfortable confronting the offending staff members.

Finally, Angela decided to bring the issue to her supervisor. She was careful to focus on organizational morale and productivity impacts as much as her own discomfort. As a result, the organization initiated training on team dynamics, which inspired awareness and some relief from the toxic atmosphere.

The change was short-lived, and Angela resolved to make a move. She set her alarm to wake up 30 minutes earlier to meditate and journal each day. She reflected on her strengths and animators. She strategized about making a move and identified her buckets of opportunity, all in the healthcare field. Based on that, she made an initial list of organizations of interest and people who could advise her. To avoid raising concerns at her current work, she needed to search confidentially. As she contacted people for advice, she started each conversation with the question, "Would you be willing to talk with me in confidence?"

Angela was surprised at how willing people were to talk with her and keep her confidence. Since she wanted to stay in the healthcare field and had identified targeted organizations, she was able to meet people and learn about openings. Her connections advised her which healthcare organizations had more positive, collaborative cultures. A couple of them were able to introduce her to people in those organizations. This led to connections, then interviews, and ultimately to a seamless transition to Angela's "next great work adventure."

Escaping a mismatch: Selena's creativity.

Selena had a well-paying marketing job in a fossil fuels company but had come to see their plants as harmful to the environment and to low-income families living in the vicinity. She had visited one of those neighborhoods and talked with residents, who complained that their children had respiratory problems from the plants' noxious fumes.

Selena became determined to find work better aligned with her values but didn't know where to begin. She decided to volunteer with a food bank that served nonprofits working directly with affected communities. She showed up each week, sorting and packing boxes headed to families in need in communities such as those surrounding her organization's plants. While volunteering, Selena met the executive director of a local nonprofit that served one of those neighborhoods. Invited to visit, she saw first-hand the poverty that plagued the community. She was impressed by the nonprofit's impact, beyond food distribution, in helping families access other services. Selena was moved to make a donation and to volunteer.

Over time, Selena received an invitation to join the board of directors. One of the board members mentioned an opening for a marketing position at an environmental nonprofit. Selena found her way to someone who could advise her about that organization and introduce her. She became a candidate and progressed in the search due to her industry knowledge, marketing expertise, and nonprofit experience. She demonstrated passion for the organization's work. She won the job. To prepare for her transition, Selena developed an entry strategy, starting from day one at the new position.

Yearning for growth: Sally's quest.

Sally worked in corporate brand management and had been promoted to work on the largest brand at the company where she worked. After a few months, she began to feel unchallenged. Albeit on a larger brand, the position offered no new learning curve. Sally's job was secure, and she liked her colleagues, yet she realized if she didn't make a change, her professional growth would stall. She told herself, "If you're not growing, you're falling behind."

She decided to deepen her self-awareness and seek new work that would keep her growing and utilize her strengths. She generated tentative buckets of opportunity and began reaching out to ask people for advice and referrals. Most of her advisors recommended simply changing companies and brands. One of them pointed her to a more significant change, a position at an international organization. That role intrigued Sally precisely because of the steep learning curve and excitement about expanding her geographic horizons.

With her mentor's help, she demonstrated an understanding of the job's bullseye and scored well on an initial screener interview. She secured an interview with the headhunter, for which she fine-tuned her narrative of how her background made her a credible candidate in spite of gaps. She earned a chance to meet the hiring manager.

Having done her homework, Sally knew that the hiring manager and she had similar early career trajectories. She was able to bridge her experience to several of the organization's challenges, checking to be sure her perceptions were accurate. Sally's experiences living and working overseas helped reassure the hiring manager that she was versatile and should be able to work well in an international context.

Through interviews with other members of the organization, including would-be peers and direct reports, Sally deepened her sense of the company culture and her conviction that she would add value. Before each interview, she studied the background of each person in search of a way to connect personally. Although other candidates were more qualified for the position on paper, Sally's enthusiasm, ideas, and relational skills helped her prevail and win the offer. She relished the new challenges and vertical learning curve.

Answering the call to a next career: Joe's journey.

Joe had worked in finance for twenty-seven years at the same company. He was usually the first to arrive at the office and someone colleagues trusted to solve any problem that came his way. Joe had orchestrated mergers and acquisitions and helped the company navigate in times of growth and tough budget years. In the past couple of years, the company had settled into a predictable business model, one that Joe saw as uninspiring.

With his kids out of college and lower monthly expenses, Joe was itching for a new challenge. He wanted his next chapter to be more fulfilling and at an organization that was making a difference for people. While nonprofits traditionally paid less than companies, he was ready to make that tradeoff in exchange for satisfying work and exposure to a new world.

Joe realized that switching sectors, from corporate to nonprofit, would be a challenge and require him to prove himself. His financial and management skills were clear strengths, and he did not want to stray from the profession where his experience gave him an advantage.

He found a bridge to the nonprofit sector through volunteering. He followed his passion to a nonprofit focused on housing, where he assisted families with budgeting and saving toward owning their home. He was hands-on, working directly with families in need, and he loved it. He made it a point to learn the organization's business model and to tactfully offer suggestions on streamlining the process for family housing applications and training.

In a few months, the organization invited Joe to join its board of directors. This was the first board he had served on, and it exposed him to how boards engage in oversight and support the organization. He continued to volunteer, which felt fulfilling and kept him aware of the needs of those the nonprofit served. Once when his daughter was home for the holidays, he brought her with him and was pleased to hear her comment about how much this work seemed to suit him.

Serving on the board, Joe learned how to apply his corporate finance skills to the complex, different needs of nonprofit accounting. Over time, he was able to provide ideas for enhancing budgeting and scenario planning. Joe's hands-on volunteer work gave him a sense of joy and satisfaction as well as novel experiences and new problems to tackle. While he didn't yet know it, these volunteer roles turned out to be the first step in his journey to the job of his life.

After defining his buckets of opportunity, Joe started the search for his next work adventure. He reached out to people in his interest areas and worked the plan that led him to a whole new professional life. Joe took a position that coalesced his financial and operations expertise; his nonprofit board experience; and his animators, strengths, and purpose. He became Chief Operating Officer of a nonprofit whose mission is ending homelessness through affordable housing.

Today, Joe wakes up excited to go to the office each day. He is working at the center of his life's purpose and applying his mind, heart, and expertise to make meaningful contributions. The work is hard, and it pays less than his corporate job did. Some days, he returns home exhausted, but this job is the most exciting position Joe has ever had. He is thriving, much to his delight and that of his family.

Overcoming a gap: How Michelle got back in.

Re-entering the workforce after a long absence can be challenging. Michelle discovered that the hard way, after four years out of the workforce. Her absence was a combination of staying home with her child and helping her mother battle cancer.

When Michelle was ready to jump back into full-time work, she had to overcome hiring committees' preconceived notions about out-of-work applicants and their concerns that she would lack current industry knowledge or the stamina for a fast-paced job.

Michelle had previously worked as the finance director in a technology software company that was acquired. It was work in a high-growth industry. Her track record was excellent, and she could have stayed on at the acquiring company but decided instead to accept the severance package to take a couple of years at home with her young child. Just as she was ready to re-enter the workforce, her mother was diagnosed with cancer and required help through an extended, difficult illness.

Four years later, as she was ready to return to work. Michelle realized that her financial skills remained relevant but her prior industry—tech software—had changed dramatically. Recruiters and hiring managers were highly skeptical that Michelle had the right skills for the current market. She kept her own doubts to herself, but she did wonder how quickly she could come up to speed with a different business model in a competitive marketplace. Despite the help and introductions of people in her network, Michelle was not receiving job offers in the technology field.

She decided to look in related fields and to update her financial skills by taking courses while building her network and selectively job hunting. Through her connections, Michelle found a way to match her experience and passions with a finance position at a fast-growing company in sustainable building solutions, not the tech software sector where she had been working, but an exciting, equally growth-oriented sector.

Landing work during a recession: Gordon's tenacity.

Gordon graduated college in 2008, at the height of the global financial crisis. With a thin resumé and newly minted liberal arts degree in music, he had to figure out a way to support himself. The one thing he had going for him was a part-time job at a comedy club that had paid a fraction of his school expenses and was, broadly speaking, in the arts and entertainment sector where he hoped to land.

He was forced to move back in with his parents temporarily. Family and friends urged him to ask his professors and others for advice. They provided him names, suggesting he "call so-and so." He responded, "But I'm an introvert." He was doubly reticent about reaching out to connections from family members. Instead of contacting people, he chose to research opportunities online using Facebook and job sites. He applied to job listings electronically. No one responded.

After a few weeks, he decided to try making contact with people referred by his family and one trusted professor. He reached out via email, including the name of the referring person in the subject line and asking for advice. A typical subject line was, "Seeking your advice on arts careers—referred by ___."

A handful of people got back to Gordon. He scheduled phone conversations or, when possible, an in-person meeting. After soliciting their advice, he always asked, "Is there anyone else you think I should talk to?" The first several calls were pleasant but unfruitful. He grew more comfortable with the conversations and refined his narrative about his background and career interests. One engaged conversation led to additional referrals and then a connection to an actual job opening at a cultural institution—just the kind of place Gordon hoped to work.

He researched the organization and the hiring manager. After a productive phone call, he was invited to an in-person interview. Ultimately, Gordon landed the job of his dreams.

Job-search lessons from an introvert.

Hundreds of applicants vied for the job Gordon wanted. Many had more experience. Few received a phone call back. What helped Gordon stand out was an introduction from someone the hiring manager knew. All that did was get his resumé a look, followed by a short call which Gordon was able to leverage into an in-person meeting. Gordon's degree and relevant work, plus his enthusiasm and tenacity, strengthened his chances. It by no means guaranteed him the job.

If Gordon hadn't shined in the interviews, that would have been the end of it. He had to compete against other strong candidates, and without the warm introduction, he might have been passed over. Eventually, Gordon did land the job—a great entry-level opportunity in social marketing. Having benefited from the power of referrals, Gordon coaches others, including fellow introverts, to overcome their reticence and find their way to opportunities through people.

Starting strong, with an entry strategy.

—

When you start a new job, your new colleagues are watching you from day one. They want to see how you engage and what you're focusing on. They are paying attention: Does the new person listen and ask questions? Do they seem to have an agenda? Are they a collaborator and a team player? Are they authentic and trustworthy? How will they fit here?

You can use that initial attention to your advantage by preparing a thoughtful entry strategy, including your self-introduction. Before you arrive, collaborate with an advisor, your new manager, or the recruiter to architect your first days and weeks. A positive entrance is a good first start to a long and impactful tenure. Here are guiding principles for a good entry strategy:

- Prioritize relationship-building "from the inside out," starting with whoever you report to and those who report to you.

- Focus on listening, learning, and trust-building.

- Prepare your introductory narrative about the journey that brings you to this place and your excitement about being here. Include personal details that will touch their hearts as well as their minds.

- Tailor your overall narrative to each specific audience. For example, people who report to you will be curious about your management style and quirks.

- Ask questions. Seek to understand the culture, priorities, and passions of those you will work with. Capture your impressions and save them for future reference.

- Build trust and relationships first. Remember: "People don't care what you know until they know that you care."
- Beginning with those closest to you in your new role, expand the circle outward. Be purposeful about connecting and starting to build relationships with people in each part of your new work world.
- Observe deeply to understand the culture, revenue model, and potential early wins. Make note of your first ideas and observations for future reference. Often they turn out to be accurate and actionable.

People don't care what you know until they know that you care.

Taking charge of your first few weeks.

—

Dos:
- Make it a priority to connect with your immediate team. Listen, ask questions, and build trust and relationships.
- Seek to win people over in one-on-one and group settings.
- In your self-introductions, show vulnerability as well as strength to help people feel safe with you.
- Be inclusive and seek to listen and learn from people at all levels.
- Figure out who the influencers are and cultivate them. Influencers are often not those with the big titles.

- Talk with your predecessor(s), if possible, to deepen your understanding of challenges and opportunities.
- Record your first impressions, but don't act on them yet.
- Crowd-source and carry forward good ideas and traditions.
- Invite and remain receptive to advice and ideas.

Dont's:
- Don't reveal an aggressive vision or agenda. If you or those who hired you have an agenda, hold it close to your chest until you have listened, built trust, and familiarized yourself with the culture of the workplace. Most people's instinct is to resist an agenda created without their input.
- Don't alienate or take the long-tenured individuals for granted.
- Don't assume you fully understand the business model, the organization's nuances, or the way forward.

Let's look at how Selena took charge. She won the job of her dreams as a program manager for an environmental non-profit working on issues related to climate change. Based on what she learned at her former job in the fossil fuels industry, plus her understanding of toxic sites and low-income communities, she was hired as a manager of community resilience programs. Before accepting the position, Selena made sure to meet her supervisor, teammates, and direct reports. She realized that her background at a company known as a polluter would hamper her acceptance.

In her self-introductions, Selena proactively shared her reasons for departing that industry, her passion for the mission of her new organization, and her field-level experience with communities in the vicinity of plants. She expressed the hope that her industry knowledge would make her more effective in advancing advocacy and community organizing strategies. She asked questions, met with people across the organization, and planned visits to program sites and target communities.

Prior to starting, Selena made it a point to contact several future colleagues and spent significant time studying the website and briefing materials, including the organization chart. She started on day one with basic information about the people and the work. She was fully prepared and excited to engage with her new colleagues. Prior to starting, she collaborated with her future manager and laid out a basic entry plan. Notice how Selena planned her first days and weeks "from the inside out," first prioritizing her direct reports and close associates, followed by people on other teams, and later, with people at other organizations.

An entry plan is a start and will likely require modification. If you take the time to develop it, you have a solid roadmap to lead you in the right direction.

Selena arrived at her new job excited and confident, but definitely not cocky. She knew that relationships matter most, and she had a game plan. Several years and a couple of promotions later, she is still working in a job she loves.

Navigating if your predecessor was beloved.

—

The arrival of someone new to the organization means there will be at least some change, and change is stressful for the current staff. When you are following a well-loved or

Selena's entry plan.

Key Dates+ Audiences	Day One	Month One	Months 2-3	Months 4-6
Staff meetings: First Tuesdays	Meet one-on-one with direct reports	Email note to staff and colleagues	Initiate regular comms and meetings	6-month goal check-in with manager
Direct report meetings: · Team each Monday · Weekly one-on-ones **Department meetings:** Third Thursdays	Team intro: in-person and virtual Meet with manager Walk the halls Welcome reception	Set three-month and six-month goals All-staff department meeting	Broaden engagement: · Field site visits · First donor calls · Peer lunches	Facilitate team planning retreat Co-create strategic plan
Peer program managers		Meet, get to know interests and goals	Engage peers: how can we collaborate better?	Incorporate peer feedback in plan
Field-based team members	Meet virtually	Visit a field site with staff	Visit remaining field sites.	Reconnect and plan with field team members
Fundraising team/donors	Call and set date to meet	Meet team lead, learn about plans and donors	Donor call with fundraising colleague	
Peer organizations		Follow up warm introduction	Meet others in the sector	Initiate a meeting with sector peers

long-serving predecessor, this is particularly true. Team members may have an established view of how things should be organized and run. Part of your challenge is to quickly absorb the cultural dynamics and business realities of the organization and to create a safe and open environment that leads to understanding and trust.

Here's how to ease your way in:

- Communicate your desire to learn the history, the successes and failures, and what's important to the group and each individual. Ask questions and listen to understand. People respond to authentic interest.

- Recognize and build on positive legacies. Find out what people appreciate about your predecessor, what was missing, and what approaches or traditions to bring forward. If you celebrate the valuable aspects of your predecessor's tenure, you will encounter less resistance to other changes.

- Avoid making assumptions. Ask questions even when you think you understand and over-communicate in the first few months.

- Take time to establish trust before sharing too many of your own ideas. Identify potential common ground and expand from that.

- Shine a light on elephants and sacred cows. Address these without judgment, but with a desire to understand the context, increase transparency, and foster shared problem-solving.

Dealing with unexpected disappointment.
—

Often in a hiring process, the headhunter and hiring team focus on the positives and opportunities. Even if they mention challenges, the depth of those won't be apparent until you begin. If despite pre-hire diligence and probing, the challenges or the culture are significantly worse than anticipated, have an open conversation with the hiring manager about your observations. Enlist your supervisor's help in assessing what's happening, considering solutions, and mitigating serious issues.

If the situation is such that expectations cannot be met or too much needs to change for you to succeed, try to re-set expectations within the first month or two. In the worst case scenario, if the job is utterly not what was represented and not what you want to do, a gracious early exit may be your best option.

Exiting graciously.
—

When it's time to leave your job, no matter the reason, do it respectfully, professionally, and graciously. No matter how long a job lasts or how significant it has been, remember that your reputation matters and relationships can last forever. Among many good reasons for maintaining good relationships is that future hiring organizations will contact your current colleagues to learn about your competence and personality.

Give your current organization enough time to prepare to cover your key responsibilities after you depart. The amount of notice you give can be a few weeks or longer depending on your role and tenure, organizational policies, or contract specifications. Regardless of why you're leaving, be loyal to the organization that has helped prepare you for your next adventure. Stay in touch. Know who will serve as a reference for a future move and have their best interests in mind for talent and other referrals.

Building your legacy.

—

Over the thirty plus years of an average career, each of your jobs can be joyful and compelling for that season of your life. Cumulatively, they are a time to grow and be a difference maker while also engaging in building a full life outside of work: raising a family, volunteering, fitness, friends, and traveling.

As you build your career, hiring outstanding talent and helping others grow are important elements of your legacy. By consciously supporting and mentoring others, beginning in the early stages of your career, you elevate your organization and yourself. The phrase "lift as you rise," from the African Ubuntu ethic, holds that we are defined by other people. If you help others grow, they will in turn lift others—a virtuous cycle that, in unexpected ways, comes back around.

Succession planning is another way to build your legacy. Consider who could be your successor and encourage those on your team to plan similarly. Developing talent to succeed you is a gift to them and the organization. Such thoughtful planning helps ensure continuity and sustainability.

Another way to keep growing professionally is to acquaint yourself with peers at similar organizations and to participate in relevant associations. Volunteering outside your organization, in the community and through board service, promotes new insights and relationships.

Living in gratitude has been proven to impact mental, emotional, and physical well-being. Focusing on what is positive and abundant in life reduces stress and increases happiness. Regularly expressing gratitude strengthens relationships and helps create a supportive environment. It has also been shown to enhance health and sleep. In the face of life's challenges, centering gratitude helps you build resilience, balance, and optimism.

Lift as you rise.

Leaving a legacy means building up individuals and organizations in ways that are sustainable beyond your immediate engagement. It's creating an impact that lives on after you. Consider what causes and missions matter to you. Become a generous donor or a regular volunteer. As one philanthropic individual put it, "I got more than I gave."

Choosing to rewire, not retire.

Some people aspire to retire early, and others dread the thought of it or cannot afford it. Still others thrive by continuing to work years after the usual retirement age. Nowadays, full retirement—the kind where you stop work completely and play golf and cards—is rare. Most of the time, people leave full-time employment and take up part-time work, volunteer positions, or another career.

Today's retirement tends to be "rewirement"—a time for less pressure and more fulfillment that can combine paid and unpaid work. We no longer have to awaken to an alarm clock. Life takes on new rhythms, activities and priorities.

Leaving full-time work is a significant transition that requires thoughtful planning. Planning travel and creating multipage to-do lists, coupled with family obligations, take us across the first few weeks or months. Looking ahead with intentionality is key to (re)discovering personal passions, setting new goals, and embracing a new life.

Retirement can be both a time to relax and a chance to reinvent yourself for a next set of adventures. As you anticipate retiring from your current work, revisit Rule Number 2, with exercises on discovering your purpose and opportunities. It's time to revisit your passions and deepest joys. Develop a "rewirement" plan that transcends finances and obvious pursuits to include aspirations and activities in tune with your animators, strengths, and purpose. You may want to prioritize learning, volunteering, part-time paid work, or hobbies that were once set aside. A fulfilling, meaningful next chapter includes friends, family, and shaping your time in alignment with your purpose and joys.

Loving the journey.

—

A career journey is a marathon, with hills and bumps and downhill runs. If you engage with your career journey as an adventure and take charge of it, you will find great opportunities at each stage.

Here are five ways to ensure you find great work at each juncture and enjoy the journey:

- Learn something new each day. Never stop learning and growing, or you fall behind. Whenever possible, choose a vertical learning curve.

- Develop good antennae that help you perceive when it's time for a move. Consider: How is this organization doing? How about this industry? What are the trends? How am I positioned? Do I have important work, mentors, and good relationships? Am I motivated here and adding the most value I can to the organization's success? Am I growing?

- Be astute and strategic about making a change. Be realistic about how long it will take to plan, leverage networking connections, and conduct a thorough search. Stay put at your job while you search if possible.

- Build the bench strength of your organization. Hire and nurture outstanding talent. Plan for a seamless succession.

- Never forget that people and relationships matter most. Never burn bridges. Help other people succeed. When you do leave, do so graciously.

Landing a job that brings you joy is a matter of intention and strategy. Throughout this book, we've explored the mindset, techniques, and strategies that will enable you to navigate the job market with confidence and purpose.

You have the power to shape your career journey. By discovering and being true to your animators, strengths, and purpose and focusing on opportunities that truly align, you'll find your next joyful job and navigate a fulfilling life journey. Taking charge will lead you to a career that not only supports you financially but also enriches your life in ways you never imagined.

A job that gives you joy is within reach. Now, go out and get it! I'll be rooting for you.

TOP TAKEAWAYS

- Take charge and navigate your own satisfying career journey.
- Design an entry strategy designed to build trust and shorten your learning curve.
- Develop a gracious exit strategy and help ensure continuity.
- Build your legacy.
- Plan to rewire rather than retire.

ACKNOWLEDGMENTS

Countless individuals have contributed to this book, many without realizing it. Their advice, experiences, and stories inform the unwritten rules and guidance of *Headhunter Confidential*.

I'm grateful to Gail Evans, Bill Novelli, Ruth Wooden, Sam Pettway, Dave Paule, and Ken Bernhardt for their invaluable counsel. Charlie and Stephanie Wetzel provided editorial guidance and inspiration. I thank Brad MacAfee, Beverly Tatum, Becky Blalock, Diane Whitehead, Peter and Sarah Chatel, Bill Means, Kitsy Stine, Norris Chumley, and Diane Moore for their ideas and support. I'm blessed to have remarkable cousins, in-laws, and other family members who have shared their enthusiasm about this book.

Anne McGlamry and Jeanne Hall have encouraged and challenged me through our years of early-morning walks. Terry Axelrod, Aradhna Malhotra Oliphant, Carolyn Cassin, Felice Axelrod, and Wendy Garen—my sisters from International Women's Forum—have been wonderful discussion partners and sources of strength. I give thanks to them and others who have listened, shared personal experiences, and enriched this book.

Many *Headhunter Confidential* insights, concepts, and stories grew out of discussions with my BoardWalk Consulting colleagues, the most talented and committed team in executive search. Thank you, BoardWalk colleagues Crystal Stephens, Patti Kish, Michelle Hall, Cynthia Moreland, Diane Westmore, Lysondra Somerville, Sandra Poole, Heather Sumperl, Barbara Diaz, and Terri Kohan. Collaborating with you, and partnering with BoardWalk clients and candidates, keeps the work joyful and the learning curve vertical.

Ripples Media has been a magnificent publishing partner. I give thanks for the advice, guidance, and editorial prowess of Jon Reese, Andrew Vogel, Nicole Wedekind, Dorothy Miller-Farleo, Burtch Hunter, Jaye Liptak, and other Ripples team members whose expertise greatly improved the book. I am proud to be a member of the Ripples author community.

Alan Bremer and each of our remarkable sons, Nick and Scott, have enhanced this book in tangible and intangible ways. They are the foundation and greatest joy of my life.

Kathy (Katharine Day) Bremer combines deep expertise in talent acquisition with a genuine passion for helping people find work they are meant to do. In *Headhunter Confidential*, she draws on nearly two decades as a headhunter and five successful career transitions to reveal the secrets of landing work that brings joy and meaning.

As managing director of BoardWalk Consulting, Kathy has placed hundreds of executives at iconic organizations like the CDC Foundation, The Carter Center, and Common Cause. This work is complemented by her extensive experience as both an in-house executive and external advisor. Kathy has hired, placed and mentored hundreds of professionals across all sectors—from billion-dollar corporations to mission-driven organizations. Her experience spans multiple industries and sectors, giving her unique insight into what makes a successful career transition.

Kathy's career journey began when she flew to Tokyo on a one-way ticket, becoming editor of Canon's global publications and writing for *Newsweek* and Japan's NHK radio network. Returning to New York, she rose to senior executive positions at three advertising agencies, leading campaigns for Procter & Gamble that helped propel Folgers to America's #1 coffee brand. As head of fundraising and marketing for CARE, she drove 40 percent growth in private resources and led global branding initiatives. Later, as general manager of Porter Novelli in Atlanta, she fostered a diverse, award-winning culture while achieving ten-fold growth. Her journey culminated in executive search, where she discovered her ultimate professional calling helping others find theirs.

A seasoned speaker, Kathy has been interviewed by NPR, *The New York Times*, podcasts and other media. She has served on or chaired over a dozen boards of directors, including Global Impact, International Women's Forum of Georgia, and Leadership Atlanta. She holds a B.A. in Sociology from Harvard University, where she wrote for *The Harvard Crimson* and played varsity squash and tennis.

Kathy grew up in Queens, NY, and now lives in Atlanta with her husband Alan. They have two grown sons, Nick and Scott, and share a passion for community service and pickleball.